PAIN-FREE
PICKLEBALL

PREVENTING INJURIES BEFORE THEY START

DR. TRENT STENSRUD, DPT, OCS, FAAOMPT

For more information, email Painfreepickleball1@gmail.com
ISBN: 979-8-89109-130-6 - paperback
ISBN: 979-8-89109-131-3 - ebook

All patient identifiers have been intentionally removed or altered in the patient stories provided in this material to ensure compliance with the Health Insurance Portability and Accountability Act (HIPAA). Any resemblance to actual individuals, living or deceased, is purely coincidental. These patient stories are solely intended for educational purposes and do not represent specific patients or their personal health information. The removal of identifying details is done to protect patient privacy and confidentiality. Strict adherence to HIPAA guidelines and ethical considerations has been followed during the development and presentation of this material.

DEDICATION

With profound gratitude to God, I dedicate this book to my amazing wife, Ashley, and our three wonderful children. To my wife, thank you for your unwavering support and understanding throughout the process of creating this book. Your patience and belief in me have been instrumental in bringing this project to life. Kids, your presence brings immense joy and inspiration to my life. This book is dedicated to you as a reminder of the love and admiration I have for each of you. You are the motivation behind my endeavors, and I hope this book serves as a source of inspiration for your own dreams and aspirations.

CONTENTS

Introduction...vii

Chapter 1: Understanding Pickleball Injuries............................1
    Pickleball's Popularity Is on the Rise................................1
    Injuries Are on the Rise...4
    Who Experiences Pickleball Injuries? 5
    Typical Injury 8
    Why Do Pickleball Injuries Occur? 10
    Common Pickleball Injuries..14
    Is the Risk Worth the Reward?.......................................15
    Biomechanical Demands of Pickleball............................21

Chapter 2: Pregame Preparation 23
    Warming Up 23
    Hydration 32
    Equipment...35
    Shoes..43
    Braces 45
    Eye Protection...51
    Environmental Considerations 54
    Sun Exposure..61

Chapter 3: Injury Prevention During Play.............................63
    Techniques for Safe Play..63

Body Positioning.. 67

Falls Prevention.. 71

Pickleball Balance Program 73

Partner Communication...................................... 83

Listen to Your Body, What to Do About Pain?............. 84

Pacing.. 88

Chapter 4: Injury Prevention off the Court............... 92

Physical Stress Theory.. 92

Strength Training 93

Pickleball Strength Program Step-by-Step Guide 102

Cardio...130

Mobility...132

Chapter 5: Postgame Recovery...............................144

Cool down..144

Recovery..145

Chapter 6: Injuries and What to Do About Them.................148

Conclusion 153

6-Week Challenge! 159

Sources..165

Glossary of Terms..175

Author Bio 179

INTRODUCTION

When I first started clinical practice, there was no mention of pickleball in the clinic. A few years later I began to encounter a pickleball injury once in a blue moon. Today, we are seeing pickleball-related injuries every day in the urgent care. The frequency of pickleball injuries has increased at a dramatic pace as the sport has gained popularity at breakneck speed.

Pickleball is a sport, not just a hobby, and with any sporting activity comes some level of risk of injury to the musculoskel-etal system (bones, joints, muscles, and connective tissue). Fortunately, there is much that can be done from a preventa-tive perspective to mitigate that risk.

My training as a Doctor of Physical Therapy (DPT), Board-Certified Orthopedic Clinical Specialist (OCS), a Certified Strength and Conditioning Specialist (CSCS), and an avid pickleball athlete has given me a uniquely skilled perspective into the mobility, strength, and performance demands of the sport of pickleball.

With the internet, we can access extensive information on any given topic in the blink of an eye. Unfortunately, many of the claims made on social media posts and the content curated by internet search engines are not grounded in science and often should not be trusted. Social media has built-in algorithms that reward videos and articles that promote clicks and stir up controversy, rather than contain quality information. The so-called "experts" with extensive blogs, YouTube channels, and social media accounts are often far off base with current literature and are removed from actual clinical practice. Many "influencers" only create content that will bring them more followers, garner more likes, and may not be the information that players actually need to hear.

The advice provided in the following pages is a culmination of years of clinical experience, extensive research in sports medicine literature, injury prevention programming, and consideration of known risk factors for orthopedic injuries that athletes may face on the court. I hope this information is useful to you on your path to becoming a better pickleball athlete and that with a new understanding of injury risk and prevention, you can stay on the court decades into older adulthood.

If you soak up the information contained in these pages, and follow the guidance given in this book, your body will be stronger than ever, your tissues more resilient and you can hopefully enjoy a lifetime of pickleball free of injury!

CHAPTER 1

UNDERSTANDING PICKLEBALL INJURIES

Pickleball's Popularity Is on the Rise

Invented in 1965, pickleball has officially emerged from its infancy and is now the fastest growing sport in the United States.[1] The Sports and Fitness Industry Association (SFIA) reported pickleball had 4.8 million players in the US in 2021.[2] Year after year, the sport continues to grow at a rapid rate. According to USApickleball.org, the number of players increased by 14.8% across all ages from 2020 to 2021.[1]

The statistics on participation vary depending on what source you read. According to SFIA, more than 8.9 million people played pickleball across the US in 2022.[2] That's nearly double (85.7%) the 4.8 million players reported in the previous year and a whopping 158.6% increase over the past 3 years!

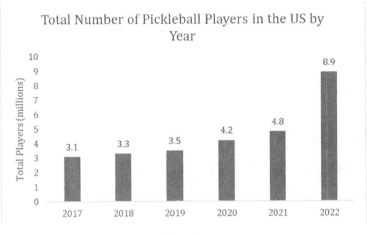

Figure 1

In January 2023, new data were released based on a study conducted by YouGov. The Association of Pickleball Professionals reported that a whopping 36.5 million pickleball players exist in the United States.[3]

Compared to tennis, pickleball appeals to older individuals due to its smaller court size, slower pace, and lighter paddles, making it easier on the joints and more accessible for those with limited mobility. For these reasons, as well as the strong social aspect of the game, the sport of pickleball is rapidly growing at an exceptional rate among seniors. This is markedly different than nearly every sport, including tennis, where participation rates have remained mostly flat over the past few years with a much smaller percentage of participants in their golden years.

Part of what explains the current pickleball craze are the unique aspects that differentiate it from other sports. In pickleball, players can begin having fun within their first day on the court. John Callahan, pickleball coach and US Open gold medal winner, says, "If you can move your feet and have hand eye coordination, you can have fun in 7 minutes.[4]" It is a sport that appeals to the average Joes of the world. Pickleball does not require elite fitness, nor does it necessitate much background in athletics in order to have fun.

Playing pickleball is convenient for typical busy American with a full schedule. You only need one friend to play singles, and most of the time just showing up to open play at the nearest park or gym will allow for friendly and competitive drop-in play with strangers.

Although nearly 20% of players are 55 and older, the frenzy is now spreading to the millennial and gen Z generations.[2] The average age of pickleball players is steadily dropping and is now 38.1.[2] Businesses are catching on as new pickleball gyms are popping up left and right. Bars and breweries are adding pickleball courts to further enhance the social atmosphere and encourage imbibement of adult beverages. Restaurants like Chicken N Pickle are cashing in by offering tasty food alongside state-of-the-art courts by creating a fun and competitive environment where players can make memories with family and friends.

Internet searches about pickleball have skyrocketed 591% over the past five years as measured by Google trends.

Interest over time ⑦

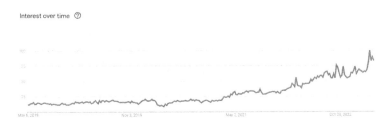

My point is, pickleball participation is on the rise and it's not slowing down anytime soon.

Injuries Are on the Rise

With the sport's popularity on the rise, so too are pickleball related injuries. In sports medicine, injuries come in waves depending on sport season, weather, and trends in popular activities. For example, in the fall, we see many contusions, concussions, and sprains/strains from football. When the cross-country season begins, we start seeing bone stress injuries and overuse injuries from running. When the snow begins and walking paths get slick in the winter, the volume of wrist fractures from slipping on ice and falling skyrockets. Similarly, we are seeing pickleball injuries happening more often with the sudden ramp up in volumes of people joining in on the fun.

The rates of pickleball injuries have now caught up to typical numbers for tennis. Over the past decade injury rates have doubled nearly year after year and they continue to rise.[5] Weiss and colleagues performed a cross-sectional descriptive study analyzing a decade of emergency room visits specific to pickleball injuries. Five hundred and twenty-three cases

4

were studied to analyze variables that may assist in diagnosis, treatment and prevention of future pickleball-related injuries.

One analysis, published in the *Journal of Emergency Medicine* in 2019 found approximately 19,000 pickleball injuries annually and determined that 90% of them occurred in people over the age of fifty.[6] Since this report was released, pickleball participation has increased by 187%. If you do the math and calculate injury rates increasing at the same rate as participation, we can estimate 35,500 pickleball injuries every year in the United States alone! Clearly an evidence-based injury prevention program is needed.

Who Experiences Pickleball Injuries?

Injuries by Age:

As I mentioned earlier, injuries can happen to athletes at any age. That being said, there is undoubtedly a higher prevalence of serious injuries among seniors. In the study by Weiss and colleagues, the average age of the injured pickler was 66 years old; however, players aged 60–79 made up over 81% of reported injuries.[5] Furthermore, 84-86% of pickleball injuries requiring treatment in the emergency department are seen in patients over 60 years of age.[5-6]

Data also tell us that falls, trips, or dives on the court send many patients to the emergency department (ED)—approximately 63% of all ED cases.[5] Prevention of falls is tantamount to longevity in the sport. Detailed strategies to minimize risk of falling on the court are sprinkled throughout the book and they will be covered in more detail in Chapter 3, under the falls prevention section.

The data I have just mentioned only includes high-severity injuries, extensive enough to send the injured player to urgent care or the hospital. One might read stats like this and mistakenly think, "Oh I'm only 40 years old, I won't get injured." Not so fast. Your chances of severe injury are dramatically less, but nagging, annoying, persistent pain problems are extremely common among early and middle-aged adults. They simply have not been studied up to this point given the newness of the sport.

These are the injuries that flood rehab clinics on a daily basis. For example, tendon injuries typically affect individuals between the ages of 30 and 50, as this age range represents the most prevalent period for tendon pathology.[7-10] This is because engaging in sports activities like running, jumping, and cutting places significant stress on the tendons. If the tendons are not allowed enough time to adapt and recover, it can lead to the development of pathology. If you are still skeptical, just start counting how many tennis elbow braces you see next time you play.

In this book you will discover numerous valuable tips and strategies to effectively reduce the risk of injuries, both acute and chronic. By enhancing your tissue capacity, you can safeguard yourself from severe injuries as well as persistent, nagging pains, allowing you to remain on the court well into your 80s and beyond.

Injuries by Gender:

Regarding the potential for injury, some differences exist between males and females that may be helpful for readers to understand. The two biggest differences are the injury mechanisms and the types of injuries sustained. In adults over 60, data show that the vast majority of injuries among females are a result of falls—75% of emergency department visits are due to falling as defined as a slip, trip, fall, or a dive on the court.[5] This accounts for the severe injuries that necessitate a visit to the ED but may undervalue the number of garden variety strains and sprains that are incredibly common from losing your footing.

Women are twice as likely to be injured from a fall as compared to men. This is due to their higher rates of falling, paired with substantially lower bone density. Women are 3.5 times more likely to break their wrist on the pickleball court as compared to men.[5] If you ever break your fall with an outstretched hand that results in wrist pain, motion loss, and reduced grip strength, make sure to get an x-ray as scaphoid fractures tend to heal poorly if not managed correctly. Imaging may not show a fracture at first, so reimaging at two weeks out is recommended.

I recently had a patient, June, who was being seen for acute lower back pain. During exercise, she asked for modifications with weight bearing through her palms due to wrist pain. Further inquiry revealed June had a recent fall and absorbed the impact hand-first. After a thorough exam I referred her out for imaging, and she indeed sustained a scaphoid bone fracture in her wrist. Once she was given proper management of her wrist, June ended up doing just fine.

After any fall, a key sign to look out for is tenderness to pressure at the "anatomical snuffbox," a narrow soft spot between your thumb tendons on the side of the wrist.

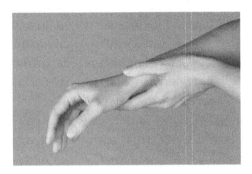

Men on the other hand are over three and a half times more likely than women to sustain strains (muscle injuries) or sprains (ligament injuries). This appears to be unique to pickleball as gender differences have not been observed among tennis players. In Chapters 3 and 4, I have laid out many tips for preventative exercises, mobility drills, and on-court training advice to mitigate risk of strains and sprains during pickleball play.

Typical Injury

Pickleball injuries can happen at any age. I have personally seen pickleball injuries in the clinic among college students, younger adults, middle-aged and older adults.

I'll paint you a classic picture of someone ripe for an injury with a story from one of my patients—let me know if you are surprised. Joe Smith, a 54-year-old software engineer, decides to pick up pickleball for the first time. During COVID-19 his workout frequency dropped from seldom to nonexistent and he put on 25 pounds because of a combination of the reduction in calorie expenditure and increase in caloric intake from snacking between meetings while working from home. Joe has never intentionally gone for a run, but enjoyed playing sports in high school and was looking to bring some competition back into his life with pickleball.

The first day on the court was better than he expected as he was able to keep a volley and quickly became addicted to the social atmosphere and energetic game play. It was so fun in fact, that he played every day over his lunch break for 90 minutes (perks of working from home). A few days in, Joe's knee started hurting with quick start/stop motions. He employed the "rub some dirt in it" strategy (as my dad would always say) and pushed on. Each time Joe would sprint up to the kitchen and stop quickly, his kneecap would scream at him. This progressed to a sharper pain when taking the stairs during his daily activities and shortly thereafter he was unable to sit in his normal desk chair with his knee bent for over five minutes without the knee pain building.

Stories like Joe's are incredibly common. Joe developed a condition known as patellofemoral pain syndrome, an overuse injury and common cause of pain in the front of the knee during sports. The good thing is, prognosis is excellent with conservative management and Joe ended up doing just fine with a bit of strength training, pacing himself, and gradually returning to pickleball.

Why Do Pickleball Injuries Occur?

Load vs. Capacity

When anyone is dealing with pain or experiences an injury it is entirely reasonable to reflect back and wonder what went wrong, and how we can prevent it from happening again. People incorrectly view their bodies in a real mechanical sense, as if we are a car that has mechanical parts that gradually wear out with daily use.

This machinelike perspective is far from the truth. Fortunately, we are not robots needing our parts replaced every couple of years. We are living, breathing, adaptable biological creatures. Understanding this concept requires a paradigm shift in how we view pain and injury.

In *most cases,* musculoskeletal pain and injury can be boiled down to a simple equation of load versus capacity. Load can be defined as physical stress, or force placed on biological tissue. Tissue capacity is the maximum amount of load that a given biological tissue can handle. Every tissue in the body has a certain capacity. Muscles can only take so much tensile force before they strain/tear, bones can only be compressed so hard before they break.

Now if we apply a load that is much greater than the tissue's capacity, there is a higher risk of pain or injury.

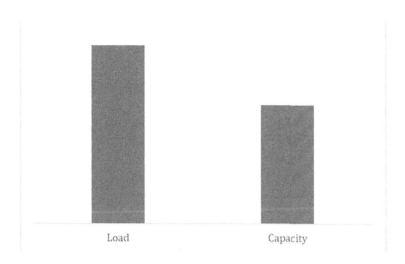

Load   Capacity

However, if we apply appropriate load slowly over time, and actually allow time for the tissues to make adaptations to that load, pain and injury risk is drastically reduced. This is because the capacity of those tissues will slowly increase—bone density improves, muscles get stronger, tendons thicker, and joints less sensitive to compressive forces.

For example, let's say you run up to the non-volley zone but trip unexpectedly and fall directly on your shoulder. The load of your body weight is greater than the capacity of the shoulder, and it is applied abruptly so there is no time for adaptation to occur which leads to an injury.

The more common scenario is someone who begins a new activity too quickly. The same concept still applies: the load is greater than the capacity. Going from sedentarism to two hours of daily pickleball will not go well. Although the load isn't as abrupt as trauma from a fall, it is still far quicker than the body's ability to adapt to the stress placed on it. When this happens, tissues become quite irritated and can be damaged. In turn, tissue capacity goes down. In both these situations the load is applied faster than the tissue can adapt.

Nuance:

It's not quite that simple. What about the cases when *nothing changes* but suddenly pain shows up? If we are being smart with our training and keep the exercise load constant, things will typically go quite well. That is until something inhibits our ability to recover from each workout. Examples of this may include inadequate sleep, poor nutrition, illness, and even psychological distress. Wait a minute doc, you are saying that being stressed out can lead to pickleball injuries?

Potentially. Having a lower capacity leaves us more vulnerable to pain and injuries. Pain is also strongly sensitized by our past experiences, beliefs, expectations, and challenging work or personal life experiences.

Again, most injuries can be attributed to this load/capacity relationship. Unfortunately, many people are being told blatant misinformation regarding their musculoskeletal problems. Far too often they are being told it is from biomechanical abnormalities such as anatomical asymmetries or that they "move wrong." Other nonsense injury explanations may include:

"You have one leg shorter than the other."
"You are out of alignment."
"Your glutes don't activate."
"Your sacrum is tilted."
"Your patella isn't tracking correctly."

"Your feet are too flat."
"Your core is unstable."
"You over pronate."

These have been well researched, and the conclusion is that most of these explanations are entirely erroneous. Those issues that do exist may very well lead to higher stresses on certain tissues, but even then, play a very minor role in explaining someone's pain or injury. The fact remains, that if we allow the body enough time to adapt, injury and pain are unlikely, even with potential asymmetries or wonky movement patterns.

Have you ever watched the Paralympics? Think about how amazing it is that human biological systems are capable of such amazing athletic feats despite massive asymmetries and compensations. As long as you give the body enough time to adapt to the stress placed on it, your bones and muscles are able to adapt to outrageous demands. We need to keep this in mind when thinking about the real cause of most pickleball injuries.

When Injured:

Try not to blame yourself or think your body is defective in some way. Don't get overly analytical about how you move. Just think back and consider whether you changed something too quickly in your pickleball practice, your workouts, or in your daily life. Understand that once you have an injury, it will be necessary to temporarily reduce the load by resting and starting treatment.

Remember that if you must rest the injured area for a pro-longed period, tissue capacity will be reduced, and less load may be needed to become injured once again. In the long run, keeping some physical stress on the body is a great thing, as long as we give it enough time to adapt.

Sedentary living will cause the body to adapt, or maladapt, by reducing its capacity. Gradually and slowly increasing activity will result in the body increasing its capacity. Increase your activity level too quickly and you may get injured. Remember the concepts of **load** and **capacity** and **tissue adaptation** as you read on.

Common Pickleball Injuries

The most common injuries in pickleball are strains, sprains, overuse injuries and fractures. Lower leg injuries are more common than upper body injuries and may include Achilles tendonitis, plantar fasciitis, patellar tendonitis, patellofemoral pain, ankle sprains, knee ligament sprains, meniscus injuries, muscle tears, and tendon ruptures.[5-6] Only slightly less common are upper extremity injuries such as rotator cuff injuries, shoulder sprains, tennis elbow, wrist sprains, etc.[5-6]

Fractures, or broken bones, are also one of the most common injuries in pickleball. They nearly always happen as a result of a fall on the court. Many falls are preventable with adherence to a few recommendations. See Chapter 3 on falls prevention for more details.

Is the Risk Worth the Reward?

Rising injury rates and firsthand experience with ailments on the court may make you a bit tentative about diving into the sport of pickleball. Even *The New York Times* cautions players in a recent piece titled "Pickleball, sport of future injury."[11] While any sport involves some degree of risk, the benefits of pickleball FAR outweigh the potential risks. I thought it necessary to include several of the known health benefits of pickleball to support my argument that playing pickleball IS worth the risk of injury for most adults (even older adults) to improve their overall health.

Cardiovascular health

The U.S. Department of Health and Human Services has created the *Physical Activity Guidelines for Americans*, which is an evidence-based publication with advice to help individuals of all ages and fitness levels improve their health through physical activity. The Guidelines provide general recommendations for exercise based on numerous systematic reviews of the scientific literature on physical activity and its positive impact on health.

The guidelines state that "for substantial health benefits, adults should do at least 150 minutes (2 hours and 30 minutes) to 300 minutes (5 hours) a week of moderate-intensity, or 75 minutes (1 hour and 15 minutes) to 150 minutes (2 hours and 30 minutes) a week of vigorous-intensity aerobic physical activity, or an equivalent combination of moderate- and vigorous-intensity aerobic activity."[12] It goes on to state that "Additional health benefits are gained by engaging in physical activity beyond the equivalent of 300 minutes (5 hours) of moderate-intensity physical activity a week.[12]

A 2018 study by Smith et al. tracked physiologic responses to pickleball by having players use wearable technology for tracking, caloric output, heart rate responses, VO2/oxygen expenditure, etc.[13] Thanks to the work of Smith and colleagues, the relative intensity of pickleball was established as "moderate" based on heart rate responses for most all participants in the study. It should be mentioned that for a few participants, pickleball was sufficient to elicit heart rate responses within the "vigorous" category.

Practically, this means that if you are playing at least 2.5 hours of pickleball per week (moderate exercise), you are excelling at meeting the physical activity guidelines and will reap the health benefits listed in Table 1 below. Shockingly, only 23% of our nation's adults currently meet these guidelines.[14] Additional pickleball play on top of this will harvest further health benefits.

Two and a half hours of weekly pickleball is associated with the astounding health benefits listed in Table 1 and is supported by high-quality evidence.

**Table 1. Health Benefits Associated With
Regular Physical Activity (Pickleball)**

- Lower risk of all-cause mortality
- Lower risk of cardiovascular disease mortality
- Lower risk of cardiovascular disease (including heart disease and stroke)
- Lower risk of hypertension
- Lower risk of type 2 diabetes
- Lower risk of adverse blood lipid profile
- Lower risk of cancers of the bladder, breast, colon, endometrium, esophagus, kidney, lung, and stomach
- Improved cognition
- Reduced risk of dementia (including Alzheimer's disease)
- Improved quality of life
- Reduced anxiety
- Reduced risk of depression
- Improved sleep
- Slowed or reduced weight gain
- Weight loss, particularly when combined with reduced calorie intake
- Prevention of weight regain following initial weight loss
- Improved bone health
- Improved physical function
- Lower risk of falls (older adults)
- Lower risk of fall-related injuries (older adults)

Table reprinted from Physical Activity Guidelines for Americans Table 2-1[12]

Read that list one more time. It is simply amazing what getting in a few hours on the court per week can do for your body. Plain and simple, people who play pickleball, or take part in similar exercise habits, live longer and healthier lives. They have lower risk of metabolic disorders, cancers, and cardiovascular diseases including serious cardiac events. Additionally, they report less stress, improved sleep, and enhanced quality of life.

Pickleball and Aging

Those who play pickleball age better than their sedentary counterparts. Weight bearing exercise is shown to have a strong influence on supporting bone mineral density, which will reduce rates of fractures, and stress fractures as we age. Regular physical activity lowers the risk of falls in older adults. Pickleball can be used as a medication for fear of falling; one of the most common reasons for older adults to avoid exercise and avoid participating in the community. Exercise is also exceptionally good medicine for your brain. Regular exercise improves cognitive functioning and is now known to reduce the risk for dementia, including Alzheimer's disease.[12]

Weight loss

As we age, our metabolism naturally slows down making it increasingly important to watch our caloric intake. It's worth noting that studies have found that one hour of pickleball can result in an average energy expenditure of ~355 kcal, which surpasses the calories burned by fast walking by approximately 25%.[13] Not to mention it is much more fun! Pickleball can serve as a highly beneficial complement to dietary modifications when it comes to weight loss efforts.

Psychosocial health benefits

In recent years, there has been an increased emphasis on mental health, specifically around anxiety and depression. According to the World Health Organization (WHO), depression is the leading cause of disability, affecting more that 264 million people.[15] A recent study in the *American Journal of Preventative Medicine* reported that nearly one in ten Americans are battling with depression and that the prevalence of depression has been increasing over the past decade.[16]

The COVID-19 pandemic has also had a significant impact on mental health, with many individuals experiencing increased levels of stress, anxiety, and depression because of the pandemic's social and economic disruptions. Playing pickleball can be a terrific way to relieve stress and anxiety, as it allows players to focus on the game and take their minds off of other worries. Studies examining psychological responses to pickleball leisure participation have reported significant improvements in quality of life, reducing rates of depression and loneliness.[17-19]

Unfortunately, loneliness and social isolation is exceedingly common among older individuals. Rates are so high that it has led some public health officials to refer to these as the next "vital signs" for older adults.[20] The research is clear—loneliness and social isolation have profound negative effects on health, mental health, and mortality for all adults.[21] Lonely people are 50% more likely to die prematurely.[22] Loneliness is so negatively impactful on our health; it has been compared by some authors to have the same risk of mortality compared to smoking 15 cigarettes per day.[22-23]

Pickleball offers a potential antidote to loneliness and social isolation. One study suggests that the social benefits from pickleball are particularly helpful during the transition period to retirement years, boosting social connection when work friends are gone.[24] The social culture of pickleball is inclusive, friendly, and supportive. Players typically show a positive attitude and are welcoming to new players, regardless of their skill level. Players are encouraged to socialize and interact with one another before, during, and after games, creating a sense of community and camaraderie.

As a doubles game, players need to work in pairs to win, fostering teamwork and communication skills. The sport promotes good sportsmanship, with players often offering encouragement and support to their partners and opponents alike. The psychological and social benefits of pickleball have been highly studied, making up over half of all current scientific literature to date on the topic. There is no debate, the social culture of pickleball is immensely helpful in improving overall health, promoting successful aging, and fostering a sense of belonging and connection among its players.[18-19, 25-26] This is one of the primary reasons the sport of pickleball has become so popular.

Exercise is medicine and the research shows that those who play pickleball consistently demonstrate improved personal wellbeing, higher life satisfaction, reduced depression, reduced stress, and higher levels of happiness.[27] Don't be surprised if you start seeing doctors prescribing pickleball to their patients in the near future!

Biomechanical Demands of Pickleball

Like any sport, pickleball has specific biomechanical demands that players must meet to perform at their best and avoid injury. The sport requires sufficient mobility, adequate strength, and tolerance for agility movements.

Racket sports like pickleball require mobility, or range of motion of our joints in order to be played with ease and without risk of injury. It's important to maintain mobility of all of the joints of our body in order to age well, but the demands of pickleball are specific to some joints more than others. Key areas of concern for pickleball include the ankles, knees, hips, wrists, and shoulders. You can probably imagine that if your knees and ankles don't bend sufficiently to perform a squatting motion, getting low for a ground stroke or a dink might be problematic.

In addition to mobility, pickleball also places demands on the muscles of the upper and lower body. Players must be able to generate power through their core and shoulder muscles to hit the ball with speed and accuracy. Players must also be able to generate explosive power when lunging for a shot or quickly recovering after a change of direction. This requires lower body strength to push off the toes, forcefully extend the knees and hips, and absorb impact during landings, squats and lunges.

One of the main physical demands of pickleball is agility. Players must be able to move quickly and change direction at a moment's notice to reach the ball and return it to their opponent. This requires a combination of balance, coordination, and footwork as well as impact tolerance for the joints of the lower body.

Another important physical demand in pickleball is hand-eye coordination. Players must be able to track the ball and make split-second decisions about where and how to hit it. This requires precise timing, coordination and accuracy.

Finally, pickleball also requires endurance. Matches are only played to 11 points but can sometimes become quite lengthy, particularly when players are skilled. Players must be able to maintain their physical and mental energy throughout the game. This requires proper conditioning and hydration, as well as mental focus and concentration.

These specific biomechanical and physical demands on pickleball players have informed the recommendations in this book regarding conditioning. Agility, balance, hand-eye coordination, upper and lower body strength, and endurance are all crucial factors for success in this game. By focusing on these areas and incorporating appropriate training and conditioning, players can improve their performance and reduce their risk of injury.

CHAPTER 2

PREGAME PREPARATION

Warming Up

Pickleballers are famous for skipping warm-ups and simply jumping right into their first game. This strategy may work for some, but adding a brief warm up is worth it on many levels. Warming up before playing pickleball has several benefits, including:

- **Increased blood flow.** Warming up increases blood flow to the muscles, which helps to deliver oxygen and nutrients to the working muscles and prepares them for activity.
- **Improved flexibility and mobility.** Warming up helps to increase the range of motion of the joints and improves flexibility, making it easier to move and reducing the risk of injury.
- **Enhanced neuromuscular control.** Warming up helps to improve the connection between the nervous system and the muscles, improving the body's ability to coordinate movements and respond to stimuli. Think reaction speed volleying at the kitchen.

- **Reduced risk of injury.** Warming up can help to reduce the risk of injury by preparing the body for the demands of pickleball.
- **Improved performance.** Warming up can help to improve performance by enhancing the body's ability to generate force, move more efficiently, and react more quickly.

As of now, there is no standard, one-size-fits-all pickleball warm-up routine that has been scientifically proven to prevent injuries. While warming up before any physical activity is essential for injury prevention, the best warm-up for pickleball players may vary depending on factors such as age, fitness level, and injury history. A good warm-up should include a combination of cardiovascular exercise, dynamic stretching, and sport-specific movements to prepare the body for the demands of the activity.

Below is my general recommendation for a dynamic warm-up before play. The time commitment should be less than 10 minutes. Begin with these dynamic stretches performed the length of a pickleball court, followed by sport-specific pickleball drills with a partner.

1. **Jog down, backpedal back, do this twice.** Run the length of a pickleball court, run backwards on the way back and repeat.

2. **High knees.** Lightly jog with quick small steps bringing your knees up to waist height each time. Swing your arms in rhythm with your leg movements down the length of the pickleball court and back.

3. **Butt kickers.** Lightly jog and try to kick your buttocks with your heels as you go down the length of the pickleball court and back.

4. **Lateral shuffles.** In a mini-squat position, move your feet in a small, quick, side-to-side motion as you traverse the length of the court. Face the same direction as you return, leading with the opposite leg.

5. **Skips.** Skip forward driving your knee up each time you jump as you swing your opposite arm up overhead.

6. **Walking lunges.** Take a long step forward into a lunge position with your knees bent at 90-degree angles. Raise yourself up and lunge forward on your other

leg without letting your foot touch the ground in between. Continue the length of the court.

7. **Open & close the gate.** Start on one leg and lift the other knee up to waist level. Rotate that hip out to the side as far as possible (open the gate) and lower foot down to the ground. Reverse the movement by bringing the leg back (close the gate). Step forward and repeat on the opposite side.

8. **Discos high and low.** With both feet facing forward, reach cross-body with your right arm in a 45-degree angle upward as high as possible while your body twists to the left. While reaching, pivot your right foot inward. Your left foot will remain facing forward, similar to a golf swing. Return to starting position and repeat 10 times. Perform the opposite movement reaching with your left hand 10 times. For a low disco, leg movements are the same, but reach at a 45-degree angle downward instead of upward.

9. **Shoulder circles.** Raise your arm overhead with your elbow straight. Make large circles first in one direction then the other. Continue for 30 seconds in both directions. Repeat with the opposite arm.

10. **Wrist circles.** Rotate your wrists around in large circles in one direction for 30 seconds. Now rotate them in the opposite direction for 30 seconds.

After a dynamic warm up, plan to practice all your main shots that you would use in a game. Get all the kinks worked out. Usually, the first few tries at these shots don't go as well as once you are warmed up. You can create a personalized variation of the list below:

1. Begin with dinking at the net. 10-20 dinks per partner or until you feel ready to move on.
2. Dynamic drop shot drill.
   a. One player stays in the kitchen, while the other player takes a step back each time they return the ball, aiming for a perfect drop shot in the kitchen. Make sure to take a step back away from your partner while the ball is airborne so that you are in a ready position before they start a backswing.
   b. Continue making drop shots deeper and deeper in the transition zone until you reach the baseline.
   c. Gradually return drop shots taking 1-2 steps forward until you reach the kitchen and find yourself dinking with your partner once again. Switch partners and repeat 3-5 times.
3. Finish off your warm-up with 5 forehand and 5 backhand drives from the baseline, 5 overheads from the kitchen, and then 5 practice serves.

Sticking with a warm-up plan will not only reduce your risk of injury, but it will also make you perform better! Those who are older, have impaired balance, have any lingering muscle or joint soreness, or who are dealing with any orthopedic injuries may need more time for an extended warm up. If you are returning to play after a surgery or injury, consider performing some exercises specific to the involved area. Working with a physical therapist or a personal trainer is recommended for an individualized warm up prescription.

Hydration

Staying hydrated is vital for optimal performance in sports, and pickleball is no exception. In a normal day, our bodies use a fair amount of water for breathing, gastrointestinal and kidney function as well as sweating to regulate temperature. During pickleball, our muscles are working hard and generate heat as a byproduct of that energy. Sweating is a process that helps to keep our bodies in a normal homeostasis, or acceptable temperature range.

Environmental conditions such as sweltering heat or direct sunlight can dramatically increase perspiration necessitating increased water intake to replenish lost fluids. Dehydration refers to the process by which our body loses water. If dehydration continues long enough it can lead to hypohydration (inadequate body fluid) and hypovolemia (decreased plasma blood volume) and can be extremely dangerous. Some notable serious consequences include:

- Cardiovascular strain
- High blood sugar
- Altered central nervous system (brain) function
- Dangerously high body temperatures (>104 degrees F)

The combination of high body temperature and dehydration puts players at risk of heatstroke, which can be life-threatening. Studies show that fluid deficits of >2% of body weight are harmful to our cognitive function and ability to exercise on the court, particularly in hot weather.[28] A more obvious hindrance of technical skills, and inability to continue at a high intensity is seen at 3-5% of body weight loss from dehydration.[28]

Severe dehydration, characterized by deficits exceeding 6% of body weight, can render continued play impossible by impairing the heart's ability to efficiently pump blood. At this stage, sweat production may cease, and impair blood flow to both muscles and skin. The following fluid intake recommendations by the American College of Sports Medicine (ACSM) highlight strategies to remain appropriately hydrated for pickleball:

Before Exercise

It's important to start things off on the right foot. Jumping into multiple games without having any water will set you up for inadequate hydration. ACSM recommends to hydrate prior to exercise by consuming a fluid volume of 2-4 ml/lb. in the 2 to 4 hours before exercise to achieve a urine that is pale yellow in color.[28]

During Exercise

Ideally, athletes should drink sufficient fluids to keep the total fluid deficit < 2% of body weight. The amount of fluid one needs to drink during/between play will vary person to person depending on their sweat rate, but recommendations of 0.3-2.4 liters/hour are recommended. This is a broad range as it depends entirely on individual perspiration differences, fitness level, environmental conditions such as heat, sun, altitude, humidity, etc. This is true for indoor play as well as outdoor as several cases of exertional heat illness during indoor pickleball have occurred.[29] Pickleball is not a high intensity sport and so athletes have many opportunities to balance sweat loss with their fluid intake. Games to 11 points offer sufficient time between competitions to take a rest break and drink water. Try to establish this as a personal habit as thirst sensation may not be a good indication of your hydration status. This is particularly true for older athletes who may have age-related decreases in thirst sensation and may need encouragement to drink water during and after exercise.[28]

Sweat also contains substantial amounts of sodium as well as other important electrolytes: potassium, calcium, magnesium. On particularly hot, sunny days, or when athletes with high sweat rates exercise for long durations (exceeding two hours), sodium should be ingested. Sports drinks containing electrolytes may be helpful according to ASCM. Electrolyte imbalances and dehydration may cause muscle cramps, particularly if the athlete is not acclimatized to the heat.

After Exercise

Most athletes finish exercise at a fluid deficit and will need to rehydrate to return to normal homeostasis. Effective rehydration requires the intake of a greater volume of fluid (125%–150%) than the final fluid deficit. 1.25–1.5 L fluid for every 1 kg of body weight lost is recommended.[28] Finally, excessive post-exercise alcohol consumption is discouraged as alcohol has diuretic effects and may impede rehydration attempts.

Table 2.

How Much Water Should I Drink?		
Pre-Pickleball	During Pickleball	Post-Pickleball
2-4 ml/lb. in the 2 to 4 hours before exercise	0.3-2.4 liters/hour Consider: individual perspiration differences, fitness level, environmental conditions such as heat, sun, altitude, humidity	1.25–1.5 L fluid for every 1 kg BW lost

Equipment

Paddle

When it comes to buying the perfect pickleball paddle, there are a few key things to keep in mind:

Weight:

Pickleball paddles can vary in weight, typically ranging from 6 to 14 ounces. USA pickleball has not set limitations on paddle weight. There are a few things to consider before selecting the perfect weight for your paddle. Generally speaking, lighter paddles have been said to be easier to maneuver and provide more control, while heavier paddles have bigger sweet spots, offer more power and stability, and are better for blocking, driving and serving.

With a heavier paddle, there will be an increased load on the elbow tendons which may place you at increased risk for tennis elbow. A heavier paddle does help to generate power but comes with a tradeoff of a higher risk for tennis elbow due to the higher vibration from off-center shots. Paddles weighing 8.5 ounces or more are considered "heavy" paddles. You can find the official paddle weight in their product description.

Light paddles on the other hand (less than 7.2 oz) may not be the solution either. A light paddle makes ball control a bit easier for newbies, but also makes it easy to flick the wrist during shots, which places high eccentric load through the elbow tendons, leading to elbow overuse injuries. Sometimes, players with light paddles will grip excessively and swing harder, which can also contribute to arm problems.

A mid-range weight (7.3 ounces–8.4 ounces) is what I recommend for most players. This is the perfect weight to begin with. From here, you can customize your paddle with the addition of lead tape to increase weight as needed. There are loads of choices made by numerous vendors in endless colors and design options that will fall within these weight parameters.

Weighted Tape

Weighted tape (lead, tungsten, etc.) is often added to pickleball paddles to customize the weight and balance of the paddle to the player's individual preferences. The tape is typically applied to the paddle's top, sides, or bottom to adjust the weight distribution and center of gravity.

By adding lead tape to the top of the paddle, players can increase the weight and shift the weight distribution distally, generating more whip or power on their shots. Adding tape to the side of the paddle is said to enlarge the sweet spot. Making the sweet spot of the paddle larger, means less margin for error when contacting the ball, which may be particularly useful when dinking or blocking. Another option is adding lead tape to the bottom of the paddle, which is said to increase hand stability during play.

Adding weight can be particularly important for players who feel that their current paddle is too light, or who want to fine-tune the weight distribution to suit their specific playing style. It is important to note that the use of lead tape on pickleball paddles may not be allowed in all tournaments or clubs. Some organizations have rules about the maximum weight and size of paddles, as well as restrictions on the use of additional weights or modifications. It is always a good idea to check the rules and regulations of your local pickleball organization before making any modifications to your paddle.

Adding tape will increase the weight of your paddle, and just like was mentioned previously, a heavy paddle does come with increased risk for arm overuse injuries, particularly elbow tendon injuries like tennis elbow. The amount of weight added to the paddle with lead tape can vary depending on the amount of tape applied and the specific tape used. However, typically a four-inch strip of standard ¼-inch width lead tape will add approximately one gram of weight to the paddle. Some newer tapes are far denser with up to two or three grams per inch of tape. This may not seem like much weight to you but considering a mid-range paddle weighs between 7.3-8.4 ounces to begin with, a half ounce increase (14 grams), is quite a bit. If you have any lateral elbow pain or history of tennis elbow, lead tape is not recommended. If this has not been an issue for you, it is something you may consider trying out, but know there is a slight increase in risk for elbow problems.

Grip

The grip on a pickleball paddle is often overlooked but can have an impact on both your performance and your risk of injury. Here's how:

1. Performance: The grip on your paddle can affect your ability to control the ball and generate power in your shots. If your grip is too small, your hand may slip, making it difficult to hit the ball accurately. On the other hand, if your grip is too large, you may not

be able to grip the paddle tightly enough to generate power in your shots. It's important to choose a grip size that feels comfortable in your hand and allows you to control the paddle effectively.

2. Injury: If your grip is too small or too large, you may be at risk of developing injuries such as tennis elbow or carpal tunnel syndrome. A grip that is too small can cause you to grip the paddle too tightly, putting excessive strain on your wrist, forearm muscles and tendons. A grip that is too large can also cause problems, as it can make it difficult to grip the paddle correctly, which can lead to strain on your wrist and fingers. It's important to choose a paddle with a grip size that feels comfortable and allows you to maintain a relaxed, natural grip without excessive strain. Choose a paddle with a comfortable, well-fitting grip to help you play your best and stay injury-free.

Index Finger Test

To figure out the proper grip width, I recommend using the Index Finger Test. This is also the recommended test for determining proper grip width in tennis. Here are the steps to perform the index finger test:

1. Hold the pickleball paddle with your dominant hand using the grip you normally use. Imagine that you are holding a hammer or shaking someone's hand.

2. Wrap your fingers around the handle. Rest the knuckle of your index finger on the handle, then bring your fingers as far around as you can reach. Position your thumb below your index finger's tip. Rest your other fingers underneath your thumb and index

finger, close to the bottom of the racket. Adjust your grip until you feel comfortable holding the paddle.

3. Place the index finger of your other hand between the tip of your ring finger and the base of your palm, in the space below your dominant hand.

4. If there is enough space for your index finger to fit comfortably between your ring finger and palm, then your grip size is correct. If there is not enough space, the grip is too small. If there is too much space, the grip is too big.

Index finger test

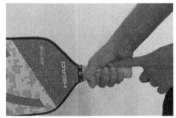
Example of a proper grip

Example of a grip that is too big

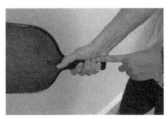
Example of a grip that is too small

It's important to note that the index finger test is just one method to determine the right grip size for you. Other factors like hand size, grip style, and personal preference should also be considered. If you're unsure about your grip size, consider consulting with a pickleball coach or local pickleball shop to get their advice.

If your original grip has worn down and is no longer the right thickness or does not absorb sweat, a replacement grip can be ordered and applied to the paddle after the original grip is completely removed. An overgrip can also be used to increase the thickness of the handle and provide a grip that is softer to the touch. Overgrips are placed directly over the existing grip. It should be noted that adding an overgrip will reduce the relative weight of your paddle by placing a higher weight in the player's hand. Think of this like adding weight on the other side of the see-saw with your wrist acting as the fulcrum. If you are concerned about paddle weight, consider a thicker replacement grip rather than an overgrip.

A Perfect Grip Will:

- **Absorb sweat.** Some people are sweatier than others. Slippery fingers lead to paddles flying out of your hand.
- **Reduce vibration.** Thicker grips may help reduce vibration, which is particularly helpful for anyone dealing with elbow tendon injuries (tennis or golfer's elbow).
- **Provide tack.** Increased tack will improve control of your paddle, ensuring the paddle stays right where you want it to, in the palm of your hand.
- **Optimize feel.** Enhancing the feel of the paddle is important for dinks and angle shots.

Paddle Length

USA pickleball has set dimensions for paddles, which is a calculation of paddle width multiplied by paddle length and is not to exceed 24 inches. Adding length sacrifices paddle width and vice-versa. The vast majority of pickleball players opt to use a standard-length paddle, which measures 15-16 inches long, with a traditional face, which is 7.0 to 8.25 inches wide. Some players may select an elongated paddle for added reach and power, but at the cost of control and size of the sweet spot. I recommend a standard-length paddle. It has a larger sweet spot, higher speed and agility when compared to an elongated paddle. With elongated paddles, a longer length and a smaller sweet spot have the potential to create increased vibration and it is not recommended for anyone with a history of tennis elbow.

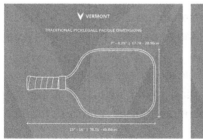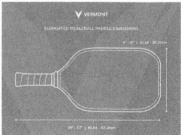

Image courtesy of Net World Sports

As far as handle length goes, stick with a standard handle length. The only reason to opt for a longer handle length would be if you routinely hit backhands double handed. A longer handle length will reduce the size of the paddle face (cannot exceed USAPA dimensions) and will reduce the size of the sweet spot.

Shoes

Wearing proper pickleball shoes is important for several reasons. The shoes are designed with specific features that are necessary for the unique demands of the sport such as lateral support, stability, and durability. Play pickleball long enough in running shoes and you'll notice quick wear in your shoes and may start feeling foot or knee pain. The upper portion of pickleball shoes is engineered to reduce injury with lateral movements, while running shoes are designed for repetitive movement in one direction. They are heavier and thicker than normal running shoes and will better protect your ankles from rolling and provide lateral stability for the sides of your feet. Increased stability and better grip will make you less likely to fall.

Pickleball shoes are a type of racket sports shoe, similar to tennis shoes, but do have their own minor unique differences. According to shoe vendors, pickleball shoes are designed for more frequent abrupt, short lateral motions on a smaller court than tennis shoes by incorporating extra cushioning in lateral motion stress points. That being said, many of the top pickleball pros elect to wear tennis court shoes during play. Either way, you are going to want a court shoe.

According to Richard Bouche, an expert in preventing injuries through shoe design for court sports like pickleball, here are the key factors to consider when choosing pickleball shoes:[30]

- **Stability**: Pickleball shoes should offer general stability to prevent excessive rolling in or out of the ankles during side-to-side cutting movements.

- **Cushioning**: It's important for pickleball shoes to have adequate cushioning in both the forefoot and rearfoot areas to absorb impact and provide comfort.
- **Flexibility**: The shoes should allow for midfoot flexibility from side to side, accommodating the natural movement of your feet during play.
- **Stiffness**: Maintaining a moderate level of stiffness in the forward and backward direction is beneficial for stability and support.
- **Traction**: Pickleball shoes should provide ideal traction, striking a balance between avoiding slipping and preventing excessive foot gripping. This helps reduce the risk of injuries caused by sudden movements on the court.

These considerations can help you make informed choices when selecting the right shoes for your pickleball game. Remember, finding shoes that prioritize stability, cushioning, flexibility, stiffness, and traction can contribute to a safer and more enjoyable playing experience.

Indoor vs. Outdoor Shoes

Shoe manufacturers have developed indoor, outdoor, and combination pickleball shoes. The main difference between indoor and outdoor pickleball shoes is the type of sole that they have. Indoor pickleball shoes usually have a non-marking gum sole that provides excellent traction on indoor court surfaces such as wood, tile, or carpet. This sole is designed to grip the surface without leaving any marks or scuffs.

Conversely, outdoor pickleball shoes have a more durable and rugged sole that can withstand the rougher outdoor surfaces, such as concrete or asphalt. These shoes often have deeper treads or patterns that provide better traction on these surfaces and protect against wear and tear.

I recommend buying an indoor shoe if you play exclusively indoors and an outdoor shoe if you are always outdoors. Using an outdoor shoe on an indoor gym or hardwood surface won't offer you much additional traction and could result in a slip or fall.

Stop in your local pickleball or sporting goods store and try on several court shoe options. Get the right fit, pick the right sole for your court conditions, make sure it is comfortable, and get out there and play more confidently.

Braces

Pickleball players may use various types of braces to support and protect their joints during play. The most common types of braces used in pickleball include ankle braces, elbow counterforce braces, knee unloader braces, wrist splints and neoprene sleeves.

Ankle Braces

There is strong evidence to support the use of prophylactic bracing and taping for the prevention of first-time ankle sprains.[31] Ankle braces work by providing additional support and stability to the ankle joint, which can help to prevent excessive twisting or rolling of the ankle. They can also limit the side-to-side range of motion of the ankle, which can reduce the likelihood of an injury. Studies have shown that ankle braces can be effective in preventing ankle sprains, particularly in individuals who have a history of ankle instability, or recurrent ankle sprains.[31] Ankle braces come in a variety of types and styles, including lace-up braces, wrap-around braces, and rigid braces. I recommend a lace-up ankle brace for anyone with a history of sprains/instability to promote improved side-to-side stability and minimize front-back mobility loss in the brace.

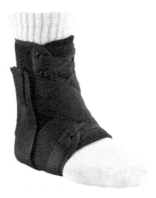

Image courtesy of Breg, Inc.

Counterforce Elbow Braces

A tennis elbow counterforce brace is a type of brace that is designed to relieve pain and discomfort associated with lateral epicondylitis, commonly known as tennis elbow. The brace is worn on the forearm, just below the elbow, and works by applying pressure to the muscles and tendons that are involved in the condition. The counterforce brace helps to distribute the load and reduce the strain on the affected area, which can help to alleviate pain in the short-term and improve function. These braces are often made of neoprene or other soft materials and can be adjusted for a customized fit. Tennis elbow counterforce braces are popular due to their pain-relieving effect during play.

Consider wearing a forearm/elbow counterforce brace during pickleball for immediate improvement in elbow symptoms that are normally aggravated by play. Evidence on counter-force bracing is conflicting during intermediate or long-term follow up studies for alleviating pain in patients with tennis elbow and is not recommended as a standalone treatment option.[32]. If you or a partner is struggling with chronic elbow pain, meet with a skilled sports medicine provider for more in-depth examination and treatment plan.

Image courtesy of Breg, Inc.

Wrist Orthosis

A wrist orthosis, or wrist splint is a type of orthotic device designed to provide support and stability to the wrist and forearm muscles during activities that can aggravate one's tennis elbow. A wrist orthosis for tennis elbow typically includes a splint that supports the wrist and forearm, as well as straps or closures to secure the device in place. By stabilizing the wrist and forearm, the orthosis can help to reduce the strain on the affected muscles and tendons, relieving pain and allowing the elbow tendons to become less irritable. Similar to elbow counterforce bracing, wrist orthoses are really designed for short-term relief and are commonly used in combination with other treatments such as activity modification, manual therapies, exercise therapy, and pain management strategies for long term relief of symptoms.[32]

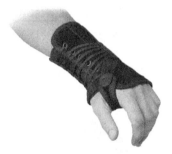

Image courtesy of Breg, Inc.

Knee Offloader Braces

A knee offloader brace, sometimes referred to as an unloader brace, is a type of orthotic device designed to relieve pain and improve function in individuals with unilateral, or one-sided osteoarthritis (OA) of the knee. OA is a degenerative joint disease that can cause pain, stiffness, and limited range of motion in the affected joint. Knee OA typically affects the medial (inside) aspect of the joint twice as often as the lateral (outside) aspect. This is due to the uneven distribution of weight through the knee joint during walking and other weight-bearing activities.

A knee offloader brace works by shifting weight away from the affected side of the knee joint, reducing pressure on the inflamed aspect and improving joint alignment. This type of brace is typically made of lightweight materials such as carbon fiber or thermoplastics and includes adjustable straps or closures to customize the fit. Knee offloader braces are often prescribed for individuals with moderate to severe OA of the knee who have not responded well to other conservative treatments such as physical therapy, medications, or weight loss. By reducing pain and improving mobility, a knee offloader brace can help individuals with OA remain on the court despite their imaging findings and avoid or delay the need for joint replacement surgery.

The Osteoarthritis Research Society International reports that off-loader braces have a 76% success rate in reducing pain, improving stability, and diminishing the risk of falling.[33] In a recent systematic review of 31 studies, Gohal and colleagues concluded that offloader braces are an effective treatment for improving pain secondary to medial compartment knee osteoarthritis and found them to be superior at reducing pain when compared with neutral braces or neoprene sleeves.[34]

If you or a partner are struggling with chronic knee pain or have received a diagnosis of knee arthritis, ask your doctor about an unloader brace. Many insurance plans consider knee unloader braces to be a medical device and may cover some or all of the cost of the brace, especially if it is deemed medically necessary by a healthcare provider. Your orthotist or brace specialist will typically take measurements of your leg to create a custom-fit unloader brace. The brace may also be adjusted and fine-tuned to ensure that it provides the right level of support and pressure to the knee joint and stays in place during pickleball play. Prefabricated, off-the-shelf versions are also available on amazon.com.

Image courtesy of Breg, Inc.

Neoprene Sleeves:

Research on neoprene sleeves is limited and inconclusive. Neoprene is a synthetic rubber material that is flexible, durable, and can provide a level of compression and support to the joint or limb that it covers. Neoprene sleeves are commonly used in sports to provide compression, support injured areas, and offer a level of protection and cushioning to the skin and soft tissues. Most studies in support of sleeves report improvement of participant self-reported satisfaction rates such as a "feeling of stability" or subjective report of "improved performance."

Personally, I am not a huge believer in the use of knee, elbow, etc. sleeves, as I feel it's primarily a placebo effect, but if you feel better and move more confidently while wearing it, then more power to you!

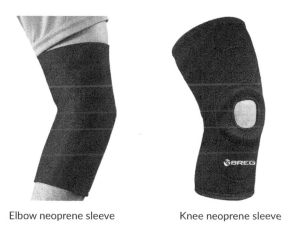

Elbow neoprene sleeve   Knee neoprene sleeve

Images courtesy of Breg, Inc.

Eye Protection

I am not aware of any stats on eyewear use during pickleball, but anecdotally, very few players wear any form of eye protection. In preparation for this book, I reviewed the existing literature on the topic and interviewed pickleball athlete and eye surgeon Dr. Michael Elliot, MD to gain a better perspective of the true risk of eye injuries and whether a recommendation for eyewear is truly necessary. He sees about 5-10 pickleball eye injuries per year in his practice and has much to say about them. According to Dr. Elliot, pickleball eye injuries range from mild to devastating and are outlined below.

On the less severe end of the spectrum are orbital/perior-bital contusions or lacerations. These often occur from being struck by the ball around the eye. Usually these manifest as swelling, redness, and possibly bruising. They resolve within 1-2 weeks and are treated by cool compresses, with lacerations sometimes requiring sutures or Dermabond. These are somewhat commonplace in the eye clinic.

A ball to the eye may cause a scratch, or abrasion to the cornea of the eye. Scraping off the surface of the eye is very painful and carries a risk of long-term scarring and vision blurring. It requires treatment with topical antibiotics to prevent infection and possible steroid drops.

More severe injuries may include orbital fractures, hyphemas, and retinal detachment. An orbital fracture is typically a result of a fall onto the face or being struck by a partner's paddle. This earns you a trip to the emergency department to assess the fracture and rule out orbital hemorrhage (bleeding in the eye that can result in vision loss). Orbital fractures can lead to long-term pain in the eye region, displacement of the globe (eye) affecting the function and appearance of the eye, eye movement abnormalities, and double vision.

Hyphemas, a collection of blood in the eye, can result from direct trauma to the eye by a ball or paddle. Dr. Elliot informed me of his two most recent encounters: one patient was struck by the ball; one was struck in the eye by their partner's paddle. "This caused internal bleeding within the globe and a progressive loss of vision as the eyeball filled with blood. This can be extremely dangerous, as high resulting pressures can cause optic neuropathy and permanent vision loss. One of the hyphemas resulted in an iridodialysis (ripping the iris from its root). This carries a significantly elevated lifetime risk of glaucoma and possible need for surgical repair. Close ophthalmologic follow up is necessary."[35]

According to Dr. Elliot, the worst possible outcome would be retinal tears/detachment or a ruptured globe. Although he has not personally seen them in his clinic, there is a case report of two individuals who sustained retinal injuries from direct impact to the eye while playing pickleball without eyewear.[36] In the worst cases, these injuries can result in permanent blindness in the affected eye.

Although musculoskeletal injuries in pickleball are exceedingly more common, eye injuries are arguably the most devastating. Fortunately, all the above possibilities can be dramatically reduced if not eliminated by sports goggle use. Proper eye protection should be strongly considered while playing pickleball, particularly in those more at risk for retinal detachment such as those over the age of 50.[36] Considering the majority of picklers are over 50 years old, a blanket recommendation for goggle use is warranted. It is recommended to use polycarbonate impact-resistant sports glasses such as in the image below.

Image courtesy of RIA Eyewear

Environmental Considerations

Court Conditions

Not all courts are created equal. It is wise to take a quick look at the court and inspect it for cracks, bumps, divots, puddles, dirt, etc. to identify any areas of potential risk before you play. Many indoor pickleball courts have rules that no outdoor shoes are allowed on court surfaces to prevent players from tracking in outdoor dirt that could result in a slip or fall.

Do not play on a wet court. It may sound fun to play in the rain, but this leads to a definite increase in risk for injury. Wet surfaces lead to slick conditions and a sprint to the kitchen with rapid deceleration may be the perfect recipe for a fall.

Be aware of your surroundings. Are there any backpacks, benches, water coolers, balls or observers nearby? Before starting a game, ensure that any stray balls on the court are picked up. If your ball gets away from you, call out 'Ball!' and retrieve the ball you started with, rather than using a spare ball to continue. This may seem trivial, but stepping on a ball during an athletic movement is a common mechanism for an inversion ankle sprain.

Outdoor Conditions

Heat

Pickleball is incredibly popular in all temperate zones but is particularly popular in climates that allow for year-round play. When in direct sunlight or playing in a hot or humid environment, there is a real risk of overheating, as your body may struggle to maintain its internal body temperature homeostasis. Heat-related illness is a spectrum of syndromes resulting from the disruption of the body's ability to maintain our internal body temperature (thermoregulation) when exposed to high environmental heat.

The vast majority of heat-related problems while playing pickleball are a direct result of the environmental conditions in which the athlete is playing. A number of useful charts have been developed to aid in helping event organizers avoid excessive heat and prevent severe heat illness.[37-38] When paired with an assessment of environmental conditions, namely air temperature and humidity, the players' risk can be predicted with better accuracy.[38]

In figure 2, Professor Yoram Epstein demonstrates safe outdoor conditions (white) that include up to 77 degrees Fahrenheit depending on humidity. Playing pickleball in Zone 1 (green) between 77- and 82-degrees Fahrenheit should be done with some caution given the risk for possible fatigue with prolonged exposure.[37] Exercising in Zone 2 (yellow) requires more caution and is from 82-85 degrees and is highly dependent on humidity. In zones 1 and 2, take frequent breaks from play, replenish fluids regularly, and reduce duration of play.

Exercising in Zone 3, or over 90 degrees Fahrenheit, is considered dangerous with likely risk for heat illness with prolonged exposure. In Zone 3, participants should really consider playing early in the morning or later in the evening when temperatures are less extreme, drink extra fluids, and wear less clothing. Finally, exercising in Zone 4 is not recommended given the high-risk for significant heat stroke.[37] The pickleball athlete can reference charts like the one below for guidance on decision making for outdoor play. Be aware that humidity greatly influences risk.

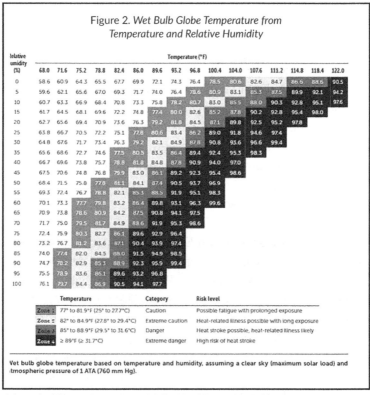

Figure 2. Wet Bulb Globe Temperature from Temperature and Relative Humidity

Adapted with permission from Ariel's Checklist. WBGT chart.
https:// arielschecklist.com/wbgt-chart Accessed May 8, 2023.

Heat illness encompasses a spectrum of severity, ranging from mild to life-threatening conditions. Mild forms of heat illness include heat cramps (typically affecting the hands and feet), heat edema (characterized by swelling), and heat rash (resulting in a red rash caused by sweat trapped in the skin's pores).

If internal core temperatures continue to rise, heat illness can progress to heat exhaustion (a very serious condition) and, in severe cases, heat stroke (a life-threatening condition) at even higher core body temperatures. Diagnosis and treatment of heat illness are beyond the scope of this book; however, it is important to be aware of the signs indicating the various stages of heat illness, especially when playing under Zone 2 or Zone 3 conditions, which is not recommended.

Heat Cramps Heat Edema	Heat Exhaustion (Core temperature 101-104 degrees F)	Heat Stroke (Core temp >105 degrees)
Symptoms: Heat Cramps— Muscle spasms or cramps that occur during or following exertion, typical in the calves, quads, abdominals, and feet. Heat Edema— Swelling in the lower legs following exercise.	Symptoms: Cool, moist skin Headache Fast heart rate (>100 beats/ min at rest) Low-grade fever Dizziness Nausea Vomiting Increased thirst Generalized weakness Feeling like you have lost peripheral vision Loss of balance	Symptoms: Confusion/altered mental status. Hyperventilation (rapid breathing) Red, dry skin Lack of sweat Organ failure Convulsions or seizures Loss of consciousness (heat syncope)
Treatment: Get out of the heat, rest, elevate legs, electrolyte and fluid repletion, stretching & massage for involved muscles. *Rarely require medical attention. May return to play when symptoms resolve, and you have appropriately hydrated.	Treatment: Get out of the heat, rest on your back with legs elevated, rehydrate (may need IV fluids), cooling (remove excess clothing, fans and water mist). *Anyone suspected of heat exhaustion should be evaluated and treated in the emergency department.	Treatment: Call 911. Get out of the heat, manage airway and breathing. Cooling by any means necessary (wet towels, ice packs, fanning, misting). Will require IV rehydration and hospital admission. *Medical Emergency

*Chart adapted from Gauer & Meyers, 2019.[37]

If you or someone you know is experiencing signs of heat stroke, act quickly. This is a medical emergency and requires early activation of Emergency Medical Services (EMS) by calling 911.

There are several risk factors making certain individuals more susceptible to heat illness. Some of these include fatigue and sleep deprivation, lack of food and water, inadequate acclimatization, age extremes (<15 and >65), a low level of physical fitness, obesity, concurrent illness, large muscle mass, male sex, and some medications (see chart below).[37,39]

Table 3. Medications Contributing to the Risk of Heat Illness.

Alpha agonists

Amphetamines

Anticholinergic medicines

Antihistamines

Anti-parkinsonian medicines

Beta-adrenergic blockers

Calcium channel blockers

Diuretics

Ethanol

Laxatives

Monoamine oxidase inhibitors

Phenothiazines

Sympathomimetic medications

Thyroid agonists

Tricyclic antidepressants

Summary of findings from Bricknell, 1995, Gauer & Meyer, 2019

Case Study:

Meet Tom. Tom is a 66-year-old male who has recently caught the pickleball bug. He plays two days/week at the local indoor pickleball gym throughout the winters in Minneapolis. Tom is overweight and deconditioned, which is partly what drove him to pick up a paddle and try out pickleball. In fact, he has already dropped 15 pounds! Tom takes a heart medication called Amlodipine (a Calcium channel blocker) for his high blood pressure. While on vacation during February in Tucson, Arizona with his family, Tom and his son-in-law, Frank, decide to fit in a quick couple of games of pickleball while the grandkids are napping. This happens to be midday when the sun is at its peak.

To maximize their short nap time window, Tom and Frank play four back-to-back games without time to rest, hydrate, or recover between matches. During the fourth match, Tom begins to feel nauseated and dizzy. His shots become less accurate, and he moves more sluggishly on the court. Tom realizes something is off once his vision becomes "fuzzy" and takes himself out of the game to sit for a moment. Frank notices Tom's gait is abnormal. His skin is cool and clammy despite reports of feeling incredibly hot.

Tom is experiencing heat exhaustion. Without proper treatment to cool Tom's internal body temperature, heart attacks and heat stroke can be common under these circumstances. Let's keep our pickleball addictions in check and ensure safety is of the utmost importance. No need to risk your life for a few extra games on a hot sunny day.

Prevention of Heat Related Illness

Strategies to Prevent Heat Related Illness Include:

- Acclimatize to the heat over several days to weeks. Gradually increase the duration of play in warm weather. The National Athletic Trainer's Association (NATA) recommends gradual exposure over 7-14 days before competing in any athletic event in the heat such as an outdoor pickleball tournament.[40]
- Hydrate well
- Wear loose-fitting, light-colored clothing.
- Avoid courts in direct sunlight.
- Avoid playing during extreme temperatures—use the above charts for preliminary guidance. If playing in higher risk environments, take frequent water breaks, rest between matches, and closely monitor yourself and others for signs of heat illness.
- Know if your medications place you at higher risk for heat illness. See table 3 for details.
- Be aware of the initial signs of heat exhaustion. At the first sign of dizziness, sit down, rest, and cool off in air conditioning.
- If you feel extremely ill, ask another player to call 911. Heat stroke and heat exhaustion can strike suddenly.

Sun Exposure

In addition to sun exposure greatly influencing your body temperature, excessive sun exposure and persistent habitual sun exposure has known risks in adulthood for increased odds of developing various skin cancers—particularly Melanoma.

Melanoma is the most fatal of skin cancers accounting for 79% of all skin cancer deaths.[41] Adults and older adults are more aware of the effect sun exposure has on skin cancer risk and tend to be higher utilizers of sunscreen, which is excellent, but newer studies are now finding a strong association between sun exposure during "critical periods" of early life and developing melanoma during adulthood.[41]

My point being, that although it looks good to have a tan as a younger person, understand that excessive exposure does not come without risk.

Apply Sunscreen

The American Cancer Society recommends using a broad-spectrum sunscreen with a sun protection factor (SPF) of at least 30. Read the label for directions on how often to reapply based on how water resistant it is. Some may need to be reapplied every 40 minutes or so and can vary depending on excessive perspiration.

Cover Up

If playing in direct sun, consider wearing a visor or athletic hat as well as sunglasses to limit sun exposure on your face. Of note, pickleball sunglasses manufacturers like RIA Eyewear purposefully do not polarize their lenses to maintain optimal depth perception. Wear light-colored, lightweight clothing as this reflects sun rays better than dark clothing. Seek shade, if possible, when waiting to play and/or between games.

CHAPTER 3

INJURY PREVENTION DURING PLAY

Techniques for Safe Play

As you progress in your pickleball skills, you will soon have an extensive repertoire of effective shots to be utilized on the court. To reduce injuries on the court, there are a few specific recommendations regarding the below pickleball shots:

The Lob:

A lob is a high shot hit over the opponent's head. This shot is often used as a defensive shot to stall to get back into position. However, it can also be used as an offensive shot to make your opponent back away from the non-volley zone. Catching a toe, tripping, or slipping during a lob return may be the most common cause of pickleball fractures and results in hundreds of urgent care and emergency department cases each year. These falls happen when athletes quickly backpedal to the baseline while chasing down lobs. If a player lobs the ball over your head, **do not run backwards to return it.** Instead, **turn your body and run forwards** to the baseline, then make a play on the ball. If you are someone with reduced mobility and don't trust your ability to turn and run quickly, simply say "nice shot" and move on to the next point. Sprinting back to return a lob is likely a low percentage shot anyway, and it may be wise to pick your battles to prevent getting seriously injured.

Incorrect return of the lob shot—backpedaling.

Correct return of the lob shot—turn and run.

The Overhead Smash

A smash is a powerful overhead shot hit with force. This shot is usually used to finish off a point and requires good timing and technique. Frequently, patients end up in my office with rotator cuff strains or tears that are aggravated by this shot. A few tips when hitting a smash:

1. To generate more power and distribute the load away from just your shoulder, use your legs and core

muscles to drive your swing. As you swing, transfer your weight from your back foot to your front foot and rotate through your trunk.

2. Follow through: After you hit the ball, follow-through with your swing and step forward to get back into position. This will help you stay balanced and ready for the next shot. Excessive abruptness in your follow-through can impose additional strain through the rotator cuff as you decelerate your arm.

3. Hit the smash with submaximal force. Think about using 75-80% of your maximum power. Prioritize *aiming* the ball over blasting it at lightning speed. This will not only reduce the risk for shoulder injury but will also improve your pickleball game. The closer you are to using your maximum force when you smash, the more likely you are to sacrifice accuracy and end up hitting it out of bounds or into the net.

4. Keep your arm straight and minimize wrist snap. Excessive wrist snap places a high load on the wrist extensor tendons and can lead to lateral epicondylitis, more commonly known as "tennis elbow." There is much debate on how much wrist snap is ideal, and I personally don't think there is a cut-and-dried answer to that question as it will vary based on individual differences in skill level, but what I can say is that heavy wrist snap can definitely overload the elbow tendons. In short, wrist snap is not "bad" per se, but be judicious about how much snap you add during the overhead smash.

5. Bulletproof your shoulder. The physiologic demands of the smash require a strong rotator cuff, particularly the external rotator muscle group. It also necessitates full shoulder range of motion. If you are lacking

either of these, reference the upcoming chapters on strength training and mobility for pickleball and apply them.

If your shoulder bothers you during a smash, begin with the mobility and strengthening exercises for shoulders listed in Chapter 4 and consider seeking an assessment from a physical therapist. Most causes of shoulder pain resolve with a conservative rehabilitation approach.

Other Shots:
Volleys, dinks, serves, sweeps, groundstrokes

Reduce movement of your wrist, also known as a wrist flick. A wrist flick occurs when a player bends their wrist to generate extra power or spin on the ball. Relying too heavily on the wrist flick can lead to inconsistent shots and injury to the lateral elbow tendons. To reduce the wrist flick, players should focus on using their whole arm to generate power and spin, not just the wrist. This means using a full backswing and following through with the arm in a smooth, fluid motion.

I'm reminded of a patient, Jeff, who dealt with chronic tennis elbow for months before seeking care. Jeff's tennis elbow resolved after 8 weeks of treatment, but during the return to pickleball phase of his rehab, I watched him hit a few balls in the clinic and realized that he was adding a lot of wrist snap to his shots in order to get more speed on the ball. Correcting his form was integral in making sure his tennis elbow fully resolved and never came back.

Watch the pros on YouTube—you'll see that their wrist remains in a relatively neutral position during all of these strokes, letting the larger muscle groups assist with adding spin, throwing in a snap at the wrist on a very infrequent basis. Reduce the wrist flick and practice these strokes regularly and your body will adapt and be prepared to deliver more power and accuracy when performing the wide variety of shots you and the game demand of it.

Body Positioning

Ready Position

By assuming the correct ready position in pickleball, you will be able to quickly respond to your opponent's shots and maintain good court coverage. It is a fundamental skill that every player should master to become a better player. Being more prepared leads to less erratic body movement, less falls, less distance traversed on the court, and less injuries. Staying in the ready position is key to being prepared for anything that happens during the game.

Back Court Ready Position

1. Stand with your feet shoulder-width apart, slightly bending your knees, leaning forward just a little. This will give you a stable base and help you move quickly in any direction.
2. Hold your paddle in front of you between your waist and chest, pointing towards the net, or angled slightly towards the backhand.

3. Keep your weight evenly distributed on both feet and your body balanced.
4. Position yourself slightly behind the baseline to give yourself enough room to move forward and backward.
5. Keep your eyes on the ball and be ready to move at all times.
6. Stay relaxed and focused, ready to react to any shot that comes your way.

Baseline ready postition

Kitchen Ready Position

At the kitchen, shots come more quickly so a different ready position is more optimal. Stance position is the same as the back court ready position, with a few minor differences:

1. Holding the paddle in a flat-face backhand position is recommended. From this position you are well pre-pared to quickly backhand or punch back any shots made at you.

2. Make sure the paddle is above net height when at the non-volley line (NVL). If your paddle is below the net, you will struggle to block a hard drive from your opponents.

3. Toes should be 1-2 inches from the kitchen line. The further back you are, the easier it is for your opponents to attack your feet. Staying close to the line maximizes your reach and allows more opportunity to attack a higher ball.

4. Slight forward lean. This extends our reach making it possible to take the ball earlier and force your opponent to react quicker.

Kitchen ready position

With either ready position, don't let your paddle drop down towards your knees, but rather keep it up, so that you can better anticipate and respond, and your reaction times will be quicker.

Returns–Bend at the Knees

Talented players keep the ball low, only inches above the net. Getting your paddle low to the ground when returning a ball at your feet should be done by bending at your knees, hips and lower back, but with a higher percentage coming from your knees. Bending at the knees allows you quicker reaction speed when responding to a ball coming at you and keeps your eyes more level with the ball. In contrast, a stiff-kneed bend will place much higher demands on the lower back and can cause lower back pain. This does not mean that bending at the hips/back is "bad" or "dangerous," it just means that unless your backside is strong as an ox, a deeper knee bend is a better option. During volleys and ground strokes, getting low will help keep your return shots in bounds and in the direction you intended them to go.

| Incorrect return— minimal knee bend. | Proper return—getting low with knee bend. |

If you are dealing with a knee injury that prevents you from squatting low, begin with the resistance training and mobility exercises in Chapter 4. I would also recommend seeking out individualized advice from an orthopedic physical therapist. If knee pain with bending is a result of arthritis, ask your doctor about an unloader brace to reduce pain during play—see Chapter 2 on bracing for details.

Footwork

In addition to fixing your body positioning, having excellent footwork is key to improve performance and prevent falls on the court. The most important piece is learning how to shuffle. The shuffle movement involves moving your feet in a side-to-side motion, keeping your weight balanced and your body low. The shuffle movement is most often used when playing close to the net, allowing players to make quick adjustments and react to fast-paced shots. To perform the shuffle movement, players should keep their feet hip-width apart, bend their knees slightly, and move their feet in a small, quick side-to-side motion, keeping their weight balanced and their body stable. The key is to avoid backpedaling and cross-over stepping as this is much more likely to throw off your balance and can result in a fall on the court and an injury. If you are having pain or difficulty with the shuffle, begin with hip mobility exercises and hip abduction strengthening exercises listed in Chapter 4 under resistance training for pickleball, and incorporate these movements into your warm-up before play.

Falls Prevention

Falls are relatively common in pickleball, particularly among beginners and players who are not as comfortable with their footing on the court. Due to the fast-paced nature of the game and the frequent changes in direction, it's not uncommon for players to lose their balance or slip while making quick movements. Falls can result in injuries ranging from minor scrapes and bruises to more serious sprains or fractures. Breaking a bone from falling is particularly worrisome for older adults, anyone with low bone mineral density or those with pre-existing conditions. Falling on the court is the number one cause of serious pickleball injury—namely fractures. It's important for players to take precautions to prevent falls by following the below recommendations:

- Wear appropriate footwear. Refer back to Chapter 2 which highlights specific recommendations.
- Stay alert, monitor your energy levels and don't overdo it. Continuing to play with high levels of fatigue makes you more susceptible to falling.
- Do not run backwards to retrieve a ball hit over your head. Turn and shuffle for a short lob or turn 180 degrees and run forwards to return a lob at the baseline. Consider picking your battles if a lob is sent over your head and you are not highly confident in your ability to return it safely. Instead, simply respond with "great shot" and move on to the next point.
- Practice good partner communication and good court etiquette to avoid collisions with other players.
- If you know your balance is questionable, start a balance training regimen that consists of static and dynamic exercises. Here is one example of an exercise program to improve your balance that is likely to be helpful. Make sure that a handrail, balance aid, or someone is near you when performing these to prevent taking a fall at home.

Pickleball Balance Program

Static Balance Exercises

Perform 1-3 sets of 30 second holds for each one:

1. Single leg stance.
2. Single leg stance with eyes closed.
3. Single leg stance with head turns. Standing on one leg, turn your head right and left while maintaining balance.
4. Single leg stance on unstable surface. Stand on a pillow or foam pad, maintain balance on one leg for 30 seconds.
5. Single leg stance with pickleball bounces. Standing on one leg, bounce a pickleball on your paddle for 30 seconds. For an added challenge, bounce the pickleball up to eye level, or perform on an uneven surface.

Static Balance Exercises

1. Single leg stance.
   Maintain balance on one leg for 30 seconds.

2. Single leg stance with eyes closed.
   Maintain balance on one leg with eyes closed for 30 seconds.

3. Single leg stance with head turns.
   Standing on one leg, turn your head right and left while maintaining balance.

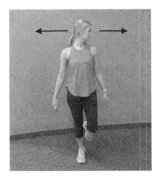

4. Single leg stance on unstable surface.
   Stand on a pillow or foam pad, maintain balance on one leg for 30 seconds.

5. Single leg stance with pickleball bounces.
   Standing on one leg, bounce a pickleball on your paddle for 30 seconds. For an added challenge, bounce the pickleball up to eye level, or perform on an uneven surface.

*If unable to perform single leg stance, try a tandem stance (one foot heel-to-toe in front of the other) with the same exercises. Once your balance improves, progress back to single leg stance and decrease your reliance on the railing or balance aid, eventually progressing to two finger support on the railing/chair, then one finger, and then balancing independently without any support.

Dynamic Balance Exercises

Perform each exercise for 20-30 feet and do 1-3 sets. Make sure that you have a safe area to perform them and keep your movements safe and controlled.

1. **Walking with head turns.** Begin walking forward. As you walk, slowly turn your head from side to side in a fluid motion back and forth.
2. **Walking with head looking up and down.** Begin walking forward. As you walk, slowly look up to the ceiling and down to the floor in a fluid motion as you continue walking.
3. **Crossover stepping.** Moving to the right side, cross your left leg over the right to form an X shape with your legs. Uncross them by moving your right leg back to a normal stance position. Next, bring your left leg behind the right in an X position, then uncross them by bringing your right leg back to normal stance position. Repeat for 20-30 feet. Switch legs, move back to the left with the right leg as the crossing leg.
4. **Lateral Shuffle.** In a mini-squat position, move your feet in a small, quick, side-to-side motion as you traverse the width of the court, or 20-30 feet. Face the same direction as you return, leading with the opposite leg.

*For detailed video demonstrations of these exercises, please visit pain-freepickleball.com. There you will find expert guidance to help you effectively perform these movements.

Learn to Fall Correctly

To minimize the risk of injury when falling, learning to fall correctly is your best chance. "Going with it" is what picklers call it. Roll with your momentum rather than forcefully extending the hand as this is the most common mechanism for a broken wrist. Here are some general tips that can help reduce the risk of injury during a fall:

- Try to relax and stay loose to absorb the impact of the fall.
- Protect your head and face by tucking in your chin and turning your head to the side.
- Aim to roll and land on the fleshy parts of your body, such as your buttocks, thighs, and shoulders.
- Avoid landing on your hands, wrists, or arms as doing so can result in fractures or sprains.
- If you are falling forward, try to bend your elbows and knees and roll onto your side.
- If you are falling backward, try to tuck your chin and roll onto your buttocks and thighs.

Remember that these tips are not foolproof and cannot guarantee prevention of injury. Therefore, it's important to take other preemptive measures to prevent falls from occurring in the first place.

Bone Density

With fractures being such a common injury in pickleball, it behooves me to include some information on bone density as it relates to fracture prevention. Bone density plays a crucial role in determining the risk of fractures because bones with low density are weaker and more prone to breaking. When bone density is low, bones become porous and fragile, making them susceptible to fractures even with minor falls on the court. This is particularly true in older adults, especially postmenopausal women, who experience a decline in bone density due to hormonal changes, genetics, and lifestyle factors.

There are several risk factors for osteoporosis, including:

- **Age.** Bone density decreases as we age, increasing the risk of osteoporosis.

- **Gender.** Women are at a higher risk of developing osteoporosis due to lower bone density and hormonal changes during menopause.
- **Family history.** A family history of osteoporosis increases the risk of developing the condition.
- **Ethnicity.** Caucasian and Asian women are at highest risk.
- **Low calcium intake.** Insufficient calcium intake can lead to decreased bone density and increased risk of osteoporosis.
- **Vitamin D deficiency.** Vitamin D helps the body absorb calcium and is necessary for bone health.
- **Sedentary lifestyle.** Lack of physical activity can lead to weaker bones and increased risk of osteoporosis.
- **Smoking and excessive alcohol consumption.** These habits can weaken bones and increase the risk of osteoporosis.
- **Medical conditions.** Certain medical conditions such as hyperthyroidism, rheumatoid arthritis, and inflammatory bowel disease can increase the risk of osteoporosis.
- **Medications.** Some medications such as steroids, anticonvulsants, and certain cancer treatments can increase the risk of osteoporosis.
- **Body size.** Small body frame and low body weight are associated with lower bone density and increased risk of osteoporosis.

Know Your T-Score if You Are Part of an At-Risk Population

A T-score is a measure of bone density that compares an individual's bone density to the average bone density of a healthy young adult of the same gender. It is usually used to diagnose osteoporosis, a condition characterized by low bone density and increased risk of fractures.

A T-score of -1.0 or higher is considered normal, while a T-score between -1.0 and -2.5 indicates low bone mass or osteopenia, which is a precursor to osteoporosis. A T-score of -2.5 or lower indicates osteoporosis. The World Health Organization (WHO) defines osteoporosis based on T-score values.

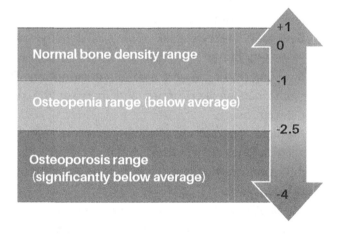

The T-score is a useful tool for assessing bone health and determining the risk of fractures, and it is usually measured using a bone mineral density (BMD) test such as dual-energy x-ray absorptiometry (DXA).

If you or your loved one is at risk of osteoporosis due to one or more of the risk factors listed above, request a scan to check your bone density levels and ask your doctor whether or not any interventions should be employed to boost or maintain your bone density levels and prevent them from dropping.

Boost Your Bone Density

Here are a few basic tips to help boost your bone density/T-scores and hopefully prevent fractures due to falls on the court:

Weight Bearing Exercise

Exercise is one of the most effective ways to boost your bone density. Wolff's Law is a medical principle that explains how bones adapt and change in response to the stress and demands placed upon them. In simple terms, this law states that bones become stronger and denser in response to the amount of force and pressure placed on them. This is why weight-bearing exercises, such as pickleball, jogging, dancing, and weightlifting help build bone strength and density. Non weight bearing exercise like swimming will not have the same bone building impact.

Nutrition

What we eat plays a crucial role in bone health. Eating a diet rich in calcium, vitamin D, and other essential nutrients is crucial for healthy bones. Calcium is the main building block of bones, and vitamin D helps the body absorb calcium. Other essential nutrients for bone health include magnesium, vitamin K, and zinc. Good sources of calcium include dairy products, leafy green vegetables, and fortified foods. Vitamin D can be obtained through exposure to sunlight, fortified foods, and supplements. If you are living in an area with a lot of cloudy and/or rainy days, a vitamin D supplement is recommended.

Lifestyle Changes

Certain lifestyle changes can also help improve bone density. Avoid smoking and excessive alcohol consumption, as these habits can weaken bones. Get enough sleep, as lack of sleep can affect bone health. Manage stress through relaxation techniques, such as meditation and yoga, as chronic stress can also negatively impact bone health.

Medical Treatments

In some cases, medical treatments may be necessary to boost bone density. Hormone therapy, bisphosphonates, and calcitonin are medications that can help improve bone density. Your doctor can advise you on whether these treatments are right for you.

Boosting bone density typically requires a comprehensive approach that includes exercise, nutrition, lifestyle changes, and possibly medical treatments. Incorporating these strategies into your daily routine can help improve your bone health and reduce the risk of fractures and other bone-related conditions. Talk to your doctor or a qualified healthcare professional to develop a personalized plan to boost your bone density.

Fractures

As mentioned previously, the most common type of serious pickleball injury is a fracture, especially in the wrist, hand, and ankle. This usually occurs from a fall on an outstretched hand after losing one's footing, typically running backwards to the baseline, but could be a result of any motion or collision on the court which knocks an athlete to the ground. While some fractures may not be preventable, following the advice I've presented so far may be the saving grace you need on the court.

Partner Communication

Effective communication between partners is crucial in pickleball, as it allows you to work together as a team and coordinate your movements on the court. Poor communication on the court not only leads to lost points but can also result in collisions and injury. Before the match begins, discuss basic strategies with your partner such as how much each player should poach. Poaching is when a player crosses over the center line into their partner's territory to hit a ball that would normally be their partner's shot. This is done to surprise the opponents and disrupt their strategy.

Some coaches have recommended poaching only when you can end the point, not simply to keep the volley going. If a player poaches too often, it will disrupt their partner's play, and could potentially lead to unfortunate collisions on the court. That's why it's best to communicate a poaching strategy before getting started. It may also be helpful for novice to intermediate players to have a discussion on who should be the default returner when the ball goes down the middle, say forehand dominant, etc. Remember that playing with left-handed players could change your expectations of whose responsibility it is to cover the middle.

Phrases such as "mine" and "I got it" can be quite helpful. Although uncommon, it is well documented that serious facial injuries have occurred from being hit in the face with a partner's paddle when both players simultaneously chase down the ball.[36]

Finally, if applicable, let your partner know about any physical limitations or injuries you may have. Pickleball is one of the few sports that is specifically designed to minimize physical advantages, so you should be able to compensate well for any partner deficiencies with good communication.

With effective communication, you and your partner will be better prepared to cover each other's weaknesses, reducing frustration that may arise from missed points when both players understand their limitations.

Listen to Your Body, What to Do About Pain?

Being aware of sensations in your body during pickleball is an important part of staying healthy and avoiding injury. It involves paying attention to how your body is feeling and responding to the physical demands of your activity. Listening to your body during pickleball means being mindful of any pain or discomfort you may be experiencing and adjust your intensity or take a break if necessary. Pay attention to signs of overheating as referenced in Chapter 2. If you feel excessively tired or fatigued, consider taking a rest day or reducing your intensity.

Regarding acute injuries or new aches and pains, it is important to remember that pain is a protective mechanism; a built-in alarm system signaling for us to take action and help us prevent injuries from taking place or from becoming too severe. Completely ignoring pain is like ignoring a low fuel or check engine light in the car while on a road trip. It can be an indicator of something that needs tending to—if you don't, before you know it, you might find yourself out of gas on the side of the road, or unable to raise your arm overhead after playing five games with severe shoulder pain.

Let's clarify the distinction between pain and tissue damage. These two concepts should not be confused as they are fundamentally different. It is important to recognize that tissue damage can and frequently does occur without accompanying pain. Have you ever discovered a bruise and not known how you got it? This is a clear instance of an injury occurring without the experience of pain.

Orthopedic medicine provides numerous examples where "damaged" tissues can be non-painful. Conditions like degenerative meniscus tears, joint arthritis, or rotator cuff pathology exemplify this phenomenon. In these cases, despite the presence of tissue damage, individuals may not experience pain. In one study looking at asymptomatic adults it was found that 23-51% of them *without* shoulder pain have MRI confirmed rotator cuff tears and the percentage increases with age.[42] Another study published in the journal *Spine* in

2015 examined the prevalence of asymptomatic lumbar herniated discs, which are herniated discs in the lower back that do not cause pain. The study revealed that among individuals with no previous episodes of low back pain, 76% exhibited at least one asymptomatic herniated disc upon undergoing MRI imaging.[43]

Tissue "damage" is not always painful, nor problematic.

The converse can also be true. People can have severe pain without any tissue damage whatsoever. If the brain has credible evidence of danger, it can produce pain to protect you from harm.

To illustrate this further, consider this case example: In 1995, the *British Medical Journal* reported a case of a construction worker who jumped onto a 6-inch roofing nail that impaled his boot clear through to the other side.[44] Writhing in horrendous pain, he was rushed to the hospital. The smallest movement of the nail was so incredibly painful that he had to be sedated with high dose narcotics to have x-rays taken.

Figure 3. Nail in Boot Xray

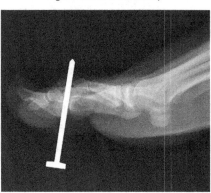

When the nail was pulled out, and his boot was removed...a miracle appeared to have taken place. Despite the nail clearly going through his boot proximal to the steel-toe component, the nail had passed right between his toes, missing his foot entirely. There was no tissue damage, and he was completely unharmed.

Although tissue damage never took place, the man's pain was very real: his brain had taken into account all of the contextual information such as visual input (observing the nail piercing his boot), the reaction of his coworker to the situation, and his own past experiences of construction workers sustaining nail injuries and inherent hazards of the job. Since his brain believed his foot was in danger, the brain created pain to protect him.

Why go into the details of explaining this? It is important for readers to know that pain is not always dangerous and at times can be played through without risk of worsening pain or future injury.

Talk with your medical doctor or Doctor of Physical Therapy to determine the cause of your pain and if your problem is safe to play through or if it will need further attention. Many times, with proper rehabilitation and modifying your activity, you should be able to continue playing through some discomfort as long as you pace yourself.

Pacing

What I've learned repeatedly during my career in sports medicine is that consistency and gradual progression are the keys to longevity in any sport. This is particularly true as we age.

Most pickleballers fall in love with the sport immediately, and unfortunately ramp up their activity far too quickly. Many picklers play for several hours at a time and with good intentions, start playing more and more frequently, perhaps on a daily basis. Before they realize it, 10-15 hours per week becomes normal.

Most beginner picklers spend far too much effort running back and forth on the court because it takes time to develop their shot accuracy. This can wear some novices out too much to play again the following day. For others, they do not fully recover before playing again, making them more susceptible to injury.

Extensive play can also be problematic for the more experienced pickler with orthopedic limitations such as a stiff shoulder, sore knees, previous surgeries, etc. As we build our capacity for longer play times, it is crucial we understand and honor our personal limitations.

Pickleball is addictive. Falling in love with the sport makes players want to play every day for hours on end. The enjoyment of the sport distracts from the vigor of exercise making most players unaware of the stress, albeit healthy stress, placed on our body. Pickleball is stressful for our joints, muscles, soft tissues and cardiovascular system—so pacing yourself by gradually increasing time on the court will make you most successful in preventing injury.

Gradually exposing your body to more hours on the court each week will allow time for normal physiologic adaptation to occur. Doubling or tripling the volume of play over a short period of time generally does not go well, especially for older players or those with mobility limitations, as it often results in soft tissue injuries that can linger for months.

I cannot begin to tell you how many people end up in my office with pickleball injuries that just "came out of nowhere" without a clear cause until we dive into their play schedule and discover that at the time the injury started, they had increased their play frequency considerably.

We'll use my patient Jim for example. At the age of 54, Jim is new to pickleball but has high-school varsity tennis experience. He has not played any competitive sports in over 15 years but stays in shape with regular cardiovascular exercise. Jim came to me with right shoulder pain during overhead smashes. He is a skilled player who has never had shoulder pain with any racket sports in the past. He has good technique, shoulder strength, and mobility. After asking more details about his frequency of play, particularly around changes made near the time of injury, some key data points were revealed.

Jim's Pre-Injury Play Schedule:	Jim's Post-Injury Schedule:
• Monday/Wednesday open play at the local gym • 5 to 10-minute rest between games. • 3.0-4.0 DUPR competition	• Monday open play at the local gym ○ 5 to 10-minute rest between games. ○ 3.0-4.0 DUPR competition • Wednesday court reservation with friends 3.5-4.0 DUPR ratings • Thursday night league 4.0+ DUPR • Regular weekend play 0-2 days depending on schedule

Not only did Jim more than double his total number of hours playing each week, but he also ramped up the vigor of play by playing against more experienced competitors. In this case, the true culprit of his shoulder pain was the rapid volume and intensity increase, and his shoulder cuff tendons were the victim. Jim ended up doing just fine by scaling back for a bit, building up his shoulder strength, and then gradually returning to high level play over a series of weeks.

So how quickly can you progress? That is a tricky question, and the honest answer is: it depends. It depends on your activity level at baseline, general strength and conditioning status, your age, your tissue integrity, comorbidities, etc. If you have historically had trouble with ramping up walking volume, increasing weight in the gym, or starting up new hobbies, then pickleball progression may need to go a bit slower for you. If you are young and healthy, you can most likely jump from playing two to four days per week without a problem. If you are overweight, deal with intermittent knee soreness, and have coexisting musculoskeletal problems, going from two to three days/week may be challenging, and you might need to play for shorter durations for a bit until your body has acclimated to three days/week.

The good news is that even in completely inactive people, *gradual progression over time* to relatively moderate-intensity activity (pickleball) has very low risk of bone, muscle, or joint injuries and no known risk of sudden cardiac events.[12]

CHAPTER 4

INJURY PREVENTION OFF THE COURT

Physical Stress Theory

The crux of injury prevention lies in off-the-court training. Off-court training allows athletes to build strength, flexibility, and endurance necessary for injury prevention. It is in my opinion the most important aspect in the prevention of pickleball injuries. Ideal off-court training involves a wide range of exercises and routines that target specific muscle groups and improve overall fitness. By engaging in off-court training, pickleball athletes can reduce their risk of getting injured during gameplay by strengthening the muscles that support their joints, improving their range of motion, and enhancing their balance and coordination.

Physical stress theory, also known as the general adaptation syndrome, is a concept that describes how the body responds to stress.[45] According to this principle, when the body is exposed to a stressor, such as a physical challenge, it goes through stages of adaptation to make our tissues more resilient to the load placed upon it. Regular exposure to physical stress from exercise leads to increased tissue resilience and adaptation. Bones become denser, muscles get stronger, and our tendons become more durable. Exercise is medicine.[46-47] It is the preventative vitamin and probiotic for our musculoskeletal health.

Strength Training

Aging, even in the absence of disease, is associated with a myriad of biological changes that contribute to a decrease in size, strength, and function of our muscle system. This process is known as sarcopenia, the decline of skeletal muscle tissue as we age leading to a decrease in tissue resilience and a vulnerability to injury.[48] Sarcopenia is prevalent in 10% of adults over age 60 and 50% of adults over 80 years old. [48] Long term studies have shown that muscle mass decreases by 1-1.4% per year as we get older. These age-related changes in muscle mass are attributable to a variety of mechanisms, including disuse, impaired protein synthesis, and chronic inflammation. Regarding muscle disuse, studies have shown that individuals who are physically inactive have double the risk of future mobility limitations compared with those who are regularly active.

The good news is muscle shrinking is preventable! A properly designed resistance training program can counteract age related changes in strength, atrophy and function of muscles as we get older. A common misconception is that weight training is for young people and that it's not possible for adults to grow their muscles. This couldn't be further from the truth. Many studies have shown that resistance training, when performed consistently, increases lean body mass and muscle size in older adults, even in the "oldest old" (>85 years old).[49-51]

Consider the image below:

Figure 4. Typical Quad MRI of 40-year-old triathlete compared to the quad MRI of a 74-year-old sedentary man (Wroblewski, 2011).

40-year-old triathlete

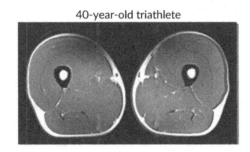

74-year-old sedentary man

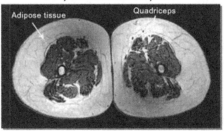

70-year-old triathlete

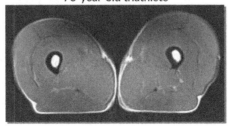

Reprinted by permission of the publisher, Taylor & Francis Ltd.[80]

The bottom image is the cross-sectional scan of a 70-year-old male triathlete's thigh. Note the lean muscle mass & the lack of fat tissue (white) in general, not only around the leg muscles. Also note the thicker, healthier, and stronger femur bone running up the middle of the thigh.

In contrast, the middle image are the legs of a sedentary 74-year-old male. With only 8.7% of older adults participating in resistance training it is safe to say this is a picture of typical thighs in this country. Note the white fatty tissue embedded within the muscle belly as well as around the muscles. When this much fatty tissue is seen around skeletal muscle, we know that fatty tissue will also be present around organs such as the heart and lungs.

Resistance exercise training has been consistently shown as a feasible and effective means of counteracting the decrease in muscle mass and changes in composition as seen in these images and as discussed previously. In addition to having better looking legs, resistance training offers an extensive amount of health benefits.

Table 4. Benefits of Resistance Training

- Counteracts physical frailty[52]
- Improves strength[52]
- Improves physical performance[53-54]
- Improves lean body mass to fat ratio
- Improves balance[55]
- Decreases age-related fat infiltration into muscle[56]
- Increases muscle size[54]
- Improves muscle quality[52, 56-57]
- Improves bone density[58-59]
- Improves metabolic health and insulin sensitivity[60]
- Aids with management of chronic health conditions[61]
- Improves quality of life[62]
- Improves psychological well-being[63-65]
- Extends years of independent living for older adults[66]
- Reduces risk for falls and fractures[67-68]
- Reduces abdominal and visceral (organ) fat mass[67]
- Reduces hemoglobin A1c in adults with type 2 diabetes more effectively than aerobic training[70]

As a result of the many benefits mentioned above, **resistance training is considered medicine**. If the benefits of resistance training could be encapsulated into pill form, it would be the most widely prescribed medicine in the world.

Practical Advice:

For optimal health benefits, including prevention of pickleball injuries, adults should be performing muscle strengthening activities involving major muscle groups at least two days per week. Major muscle groups include legs, hips, chest, back, abdomen, shoulders, and arms. Adaptations to muscle strengthening exercises are specific to the muscles used during an exercise, so a variety of exercises are useful for optimal pickleball strength. The forthcoming exercise recommendations are helpful for all adults to improve their fitness but will be tailored to address specific needs for the pickleball athlete.

Examples of strengthening exercises include free weights (dumbbells, barbells, kettlebells), body weight exercises or calisthenics (pushups, dips, crunches, etc.), and machine-based strengthening. To get the most value out of weight training and maximize benefits, some suggestions will be made regarding intensity of exercise, and volume of lifts.

Intensity:

Muscle strengthening is sufficient to stimulate changes in your body when performed at a moderate intensity or greater. One method to help determine intensity of your lifting routine is the rating of perceived exertion (RPE) scale. This is a measure of the overall difficulty of the exercise on a scale from 0 to 10 based on self-perception. With zero being the amount of physical challenge at rest and 10 being the most challenging exercise possible.

Another effective method of measuring intensity is using the reps in reserve method (RIR). RIR is a measure of how many reps an individual feels they could have performed before reaching muscle failure at the conclusion of a set. For example, after a set of 10 reps, if an individual estimates they could have done 5 more repetitions before failure, this would be 5 RIR. Research has shown that there is a strong correlation between RIR and RPE.[71] In other words, as the number of reps in reserve decreases (meaning the individual feels closer to muscle failure), the RPE tends to increase. Conversely, as the number of reps in reserve increases (meaning the individual feels they can do more reps before muscle failure), the RPE tends to decrease. Both scales can be useful for adjusting exercise intensity when training.

When starting a weight training program for the first time, I recommend beginning at a moderate intensity. Novice lifters or someone who has taken a long hiatus from lifting, maybe due to a recent surgery, should begin at a 4-5/10 RPE or with 6-8 reps left in the tank (RIR). As you become more trained, a goal to reach 7/10 RPE or being 3-4 reps away from muscle failure is ideal as muscular adaptation rate peaks at higher intensity lifts.[72] Exercising to complete muscle failure is not necessary nor recommended given the increased risk for injury and similar benefits from lifting at sub-maximal, yet still high RPE intensities. A general recommendation is to never increase the weight by >10% to allow for gradual adaptations and minimize risk of injury with weight training.

Table 5. RPE vs. RIR Methods for Intensity Selection

RPE	Reps in Reserve
1-2	Little to no effort
3-4	Light effort
5-6	4-6 left in the tank
7	3 reps remaining
8	2 reps remaining
9	1 rep remaining
10	Maximum effort

*Adapted from Zuordos, 2015

Keep in mind that these scales are subjective and vary greatly from person to person. They can be useful as a general guideline to help individuals determine RPE and RIR while lifting.

Volume

Determining the ideal volume of sets and reps for exercise depends on many factors and should be individualized when possible. Studies have shown that even one set of 8 to 12 repetitions per exercise is effective, but that two or three sets is more effective for building strength and resilience of your tissues.[12,72]

Strength development is a slow and gradual process. The key to continued improvements in your strength is adhering to the strength and conditioning principle of progressive overload. Progressive overload states that by gradually and incrementally loading the muscles, adaptation will occur and without progressive loading of the muscles, muscle growth will plateau. There are many ways to modify exercises to continue building strength. Examples include increasing weight, increasing number of repetitions, reducing the speed of movement (more time under tension), reducing the rest time between exercises, and increasing frequency (i.e., from 2 to 3+ days/week).

Specific Exercises

This comprehensive pickleball resistance training program is designed to be performed two or three days per week. It is advised to start with the 2-day program, incorporating Day 1 and Day 2 exercises. As you advance, you can gradually introduce a 3rd day (Day 3) of weight training. Detailed explanations and accompanying pictures are provided to guide you through the exercises. To effectively track your progress over time, I recommend maintaining an exercise journal where you can record your routine, including sets, reps, and the weights used. This valuable practice will allow you to monitor and measure your advancements.

These exercises were chosen to enhance human movement (push, pull, lift, lunge, squat, twist) and strengthen specific muscles and movements needed for pickleball (hip abduction, shoulder external rotation, wrist extension, etc.). These exercises will also train commonly injured tendons such as the rotator cuff, quad and patellar tendons, lateral hip tendons, and tendons of the lateral elbow.

The following tables outline various exercises, along with corresponding sets and repetitions for each lifting day. Additionally, a visual demonstration and step-by-step guide have been included for each exercise.

Pickleball Strength Training Program

Day 1		
Exercise	Repetitions	Sets
Squat	8-12	1-3
Plyometric Fall Forward Lunge	8-12	1-3
Reverse Chops	8-12	1-3
Seated Calf Raises	8-12	1-3
Seated Row	8-12	1-3
Banded Sidestepping	8-12	1-3
Incline Press	8-12	1-3
Banded Flashers	10-15	1-3
Dumbbell Wrist Extension	8-12	1-3

Day 2		
Exercise	Repetitions	Sets
Deadlift	8-12	1-3
Dynamic Lateral Lunges	8-12	1-3
Chops	8-12	1-3
Standing Calf Raises	8-12	1-3
Lat Pull Downs	8-12	1-3
Hop and Hold with Band Abductions	2 x Length of Gym	1-3
Dumbbell Scaption	8-12	1-3
Cable Shoulder External Rotation Arm at Side	10-15	1-3
Wrist Roll Up	1 Length of Rope	1-3

Day 3 (Optional Progression)		
Exercise	Repetitions	Sets
Goblet Squat	8-12	1-3
Retro Lunge with Med Ball Twist	8-12	1-3
Single Arm Horizontal Abduction with Torso Rotation	8-12	1-3
Single Leg Lateral Line Hops	20-60 Seconds	1-3
Single Arm Bent Over Row	8-12 Each	1-3
Single Leg Standing Hip Abduction with Band at Knees	To Fatigue	1-3
Dumbbell Abduction	8-12	1-3
90-90 Shoulder External Rotation	10-15	1-3
Heavy Suitcase Carry	Length of Gym	1-3

Pickleball Strength Program Step-by-Step Guide

Day 1 Exercises

Squat

1. Stand with your feet shoulder-width apart and your toes pointing forward or slightly outward.
2. Start the movement by pushing your hips back and bending your knees, as if you were sitting down on a chair.
3. Keep your weight evenly distributed between your heels and the balls of your feet.
4. Lower yourself down until your thighs are parallel to the ground, or as close to parallel as you can comfortably go.
5. Pause briefly at the bottom of the squat, then push through your heels to stand back up, straightening your legs completely at the top of the movement.

Once this becomes easy for you, progress by increasing the number of repetitions, or by adding external weight in the form of a goblet squat (weight in front) or a barbell back squat (weight on shoulders).

Drop Forward Lunge

1. Stand with your feet hip-width apart and your hands on your hips or at your sides.
2. Fall forward, stepping out with your right foot, taking a larger than normal step, and bend both knees to decelerate and lower yourself into a lunge position.
3. As you lower yourself into the lunge, keep your front knee directly above your ankle, minimizing knee drift inwardly.
4. Once you've lowered yourself as far as you can comfortably go, pause for a moment and then press through your front foot to power your way back up in one fluid motion.
5. Return your right foot to the starting position and repeat the movement for 8-12 reps.
6. Continue with your left leg forward, repeating this same process.

Reverse Chops

1. Attach a handle to the low pulley of a cable machine and adjust the weight as needed.
2. Begin by holding the pulley handle with both hands. The pulley should be out in front and anchored to the side at floor level.
3. Bend your knees and bring your hands towards the anchor point. Keeping your elbows straight, pull up against the resistance as you rotate away from the anchor point in a diagonal direction.
4. Return to the starting position and repeat.

This exercise can also be performed with a medicine ball or weight in hand, but cable resistance is preferred.

Starting position

Ending position

Seated Calf Raises

1. Begin by sitting upright on a bench or chair holding a dumbbell on top of your knees. Keep your feet flat on the ground.
2. Slowly raise both heels at the same time. Then lower them down to the starting position. Repeat.
3. Make sure to keep the balls of your feet in contact with the ground throughout the exercise. Raise your heels as high as possible.

Cable Seated Row

1. Adjust the pin to your desired weight. Begin in a seated position with your torso upright and your back straight, with knees slightly bent. Grasp the handles with your wrists in a comfortable position. Many handle variations exist, so find one that feels comfortable.
2. Pull the handles in towards your lower ribs, keeping your elbows by your sides, and squeezing your shoulder blades together in your middle back. Repeat.

Banded Sidestepping

1. Begin by standing upright with a resistance band looped around your ankles.
2. Bend your knees slightly so you are in a ready stance position, as if at the kitchen line.
3. Step sideways, always keeping tension on the band.
4. Keep your toes pointed forward and prevent your knees from caving in while sidestepping.
5. Repeat sidestepping until a 7/10 "burn" level is felt in your glutes.

If this exercise is too challenging, or if you can only sidestep a very short distance, use a band with less resistance or raise the band loop up around your knees.

Incline Dumbbell Bench Press

1. Begin by sitting on an inclined bench with a dumbbell in each hand.
2. Press your arms straight up with your palms facing forward.
3. Lower the dumbbells to chest level. Repeat.

Starting position   Ending position

Banded Flashers

1. Begin by standing with your arms by your sides, holding a resistance band in both hands without slack in the band.
2. Bend your elbows to approximately 90 degrees with your palms up.
3. Rotate your forearms out to the sides and pinch your shoulder blades down and back together.
4. Return to the starting position. Make sure you keep your elbows at your sides and try to avoid shrugging your shoulders up towards your ears.

Dumbbell Wrist Extension

1. Begin sitting with one forearm resting on a table or on your thigh, holding a dumbbell with your hand hanging off the edge.
2. With your palm facing down, raise your wrist up, then slowly lower it back down, and repeat.

Day 2 Exercises

Kettlebell or Dumbbell Deadlift

1. Begin by standing with your feet slightly wider than shoulder width apart and a kettlebell in front of you on the floor.
2. Bend at your hips to reach down and grasp the weight. Lift it off the ground, engaging your back and thigh muscles, then lower it back down in the same manner and repeat.

If you have limited hamstring flexibility, place a box or step in front of you and place the weight on the step rather than the floor.

Starting position   Ending position

Dynamic Lateral Lunges

1. Begin in a standing upright position.
2. Step forward and diagonally approximately 45 degrees to the side, then lower your body into a lunge position, bending both knees simultaneously.
3. Return to the starting position in one fluid motion and repeat to the other side.

Chops

1. Begin by facing the cable column. Raise the pulley so that it is above your head and clip the handle to the pulley. Adjust the pin to your desired weight.
2. Stand tall with the machine to your side, holding the handle with both hands.
3. Slowly pull the handle down and across your body in a diagonal movement, rotating your trunk, then return to the starting position and repeat.

Standing Calf Raises

1. Stand in an upright position with your feet about shoulder width apart.
2. Raise both heels off the ground at the same time, then lower them down to the floor.

You can progress this exercise by increasing the total range of motion by dropping heels down off a step, or by performing the exercise on a single leg.

Lat Pull Down Machine

1. Begin by facing the machine. Adjust the pin to your desired weight.
2. Grab the bar overhead and move to a seated position with your elbows straight. Tuck your thighs under the pad to ensure they are firmly held in place and adjust if necessary.
3. Pull your arms down against the resistance, to shoulder height, with the bar in front of your face.
4. Return to the starting position and repeat.

Hop and Hold with Band Abductions

1. Begin by standing in a ready stance position with feet shoulder width apart and an elastic band around your knees.
2. Shift your weight over to one leg while maintaining an athletic position.
3. Hop forward from one foot to the other, landing softly.
4. Lift your opposite leg straight out to your side, pushing against the resistance band. Perform 3 repetitions.
5. Hop forward landing on the opposite leg, followed by 3 abductions, alternating legs until desired reps are met.

Dumbbell Scaption

1. Begin in a standing upright position, a dumbbell in each hand, your arms resting at your sides.
2. With thumbs pointing upwards, raise your arms diagonally at roughly a 30-degree angle from your body.
3. Lower your arms back to your sides and repeat.

*Make sure to keep your elbows straight and avoid shrugging your shoulders. This exercise selectively targets the supraspinatus, a rotator cuff muscle that is commonly injured in pickleball.

Cable Shoulder External Rotation with Arm at Side

1. Begin by adjusting the machine to your desired weight. Next, move the cable pulley so it's anchored at elbow height.
2. Grab the handle and step away from the machine until you feel resistance.
3. Stand in an upright position with your elbow bent to 90 degrees.
4. Squeeze your elbow to your side and keep it bent to 90 degrees, pull your hand away from your belly to the outside, pulling against the resistance.
5. Return to the starting position and repeat.
6. Repeat this exercise with the opposite shoulder.

*Ideally, you should feel the fatigue sensation in the backside of your shoulder. This exercise is intended to improve the health of your rotator cuff, and train the shoulder decelerators in an overhead smash, as well as the muscle group used in backhand hitting.

Starting position   Ending position

Wrists Roll Up

1. Stand holding a wrist roller with your arms straight out in front of you. Your shoulders should be in a neutral position.
2. Moving only your wrists, rotate them towards you as the weight ascends until there is no more rope to roll.
3. Now rotate your wrists in the opposite direction, maintain control while you slowly unwind the rope until it is fully unwound.

This exercise can be performed with a cable machine using light resistance and a flat bar attachment, or you can easily make the equipment at home using a stick, rope, and a 1 to 5 pound weight. This is by far my favorite tennis elbow prevention exercise.

Day 3 Exercises

Goblet Squat

1. Stand with your feet shoulder-width apart and your toes pointing forward or slightly outward. Hold a single dumbbell vertically at chest height.
2. Start the movement by pushing your hips back and bending your knees, as if you were sitting down on a chair.
3. Keep your weight evenly distributed between your heels and the balls of your feet.
4. Lower yourself down until your thighs are parallel to the ground, or as close to parallel as you can comfortably go.
5. Pause briefly at the bottom of the squat, then push through your heels to stand back up, straightening your legs completely at the top of the movement.

Retro Lunge with Med Ball Twist

1. Begin in a standing upright position holding a medicine ball in front of your chest with elbows bent.
2. Take a long step backward into a lunge position with your knees bent at 90-degree angles, then rotate your torso toward your forward leg. Rotate back, raise yourself into the starting position and repeat.

*Avoid letting either knee collapse inward.

Single Arm Cable Horizontal Abduction

1. Begin by adjusting the machine to your desired weight. Next, move the cable pulley so it's anchored at shoulder height.
2. Grab the handle and step away from the machine until you feel the resistance.
3. Begin in a standing upright position holding the cable handle with your arm straight across your body, parallel to the ground. You should be standing to the side of the anchor point.
4. Keep your arm parallel to the ground while pulling it against resistance to the other side of your body. Maintain a straight elbow during the movement.
5. Return to starting position and repeat.

*Make sure to keep your elbow straight and avoid shrugging your shoulder during the exercise. Switch arms and repeat.

Single Leg Lateral Line Hops

1. Stand on one leg.
2. Jump to the side over a line, jump back.
3. Stay on your toes and find a good rhythm.

Single Arm Bent Over Row

1. Begin with your left foot on the ground and the right knee on a chair or bench, holding a weight in your left hand.
2. Pull your arm upward, bending your elbow by your side, and pulling your shoulder blade down and back.
3. Lower your arm back down and repeat.

Single Leg Standing Hip Abduction with Band at Knees

1. Begin in a standing upright position, with a resistance band around your thighs.
2. Lift your leg straight out to your side, pulling against the resistance band, then slowly return to the starting position and repeat until fatigue is felt in the outside of your hips.

* Ideally this is performed standing on one leg. If you need a balance aid, hold onto a stable object at your side and use the least amount of support needed to maintain balance (1-2 fingers). Often, the fatigue is felt most on the stationary leg.

Dumbbell Shoulder Abduction

1. Begin in a standing upright position with your arms resting at your sides, holding a dumbbell in each hand.
2. Keeping your elbows straight, raise both arms directly out to your sides with your palms down, then lower them back down and repeat.
3. Avoid shrugging your shoulders during the exercise.

90-90 Cable External Rotation

1. Begin by adjusting the machine to your desired weight. Next, move the cable pulley so it's anchored at shoulder height.
2. Grab the handle, stepping away from the machine until you feel resistance.
3. Begin in a standing upright position with one arm out to the side and your elbows bent to 90 degrees with your palm facing the floor.
4. Slowly rotate your arm upward until your palm is facing forward.
5. Repeat this movement for the desired number of repetitions

*Make sure not to let your elbow drop as you rotate your arm. If you are unable to maintain this position, lighten the weight.

Suitcase Carry

1. Begin in a standing position with a kettlebell or dumbbell on the floor beside your foot.
2. Lower yourself, bending at the hips and knees. Grasp the kettlebell with one hand, then return to standing with the weight at your side.
3. With an upright posture, walk forward the desired length. Aim to maintain an upright posture without leaning to one side or the other and avoid shrugging your shoulders.
4. Repeat on the other side.

*Begin with 20-30 feet and progress by adding weight or distance to the suitcase carry.

By incorporating this workout into your training regimen, you'll be better equipped to meet the demands of pickleball and reduce the risk of injury. These tools will propel your fitness and your game to the next level!

DOMS

After an intense workout session that left your muscles burning and your heart pumping, it's no surprise that you may experience a phenomenon known as Delayed Onset Muscle Soreness, commonly known as DOMS.

DOMS is a type of muscular pain that occurs 24-72 hours after engaging in physical activity. It is most commonly experienced by those new to exercise or to those who have significantly increased the intensity, duration, or type of exercise they are doing.

DOMS is caused by microscopic damage to muscle fibers that occurs during exercise. This damage triggers a process of repair and rebuilding that ultimately leads to stronger and more resilient muscles. So, in this sense, muscle damage can be seen as a helpful, necessary part of the muscle adaptation process that leads to improvements in strength, endurance, and overall fitness.

During the recovery period from lifting, there will be some inflammation in the muscles, which causes the pain and stiffness associated with DOMS. The good news is that DOMS is a normal and temporary response to exercise and usually resolves within a few days.

Light exercise, stretching, and rest can help alleviate the symptoms of DOMS, and it is generally safe to continue exercising even when experiencing DOMS. Pay attention to your body and refrain from exceeding your personal limits. Limit movements that cause excessive soreness or lead to soreness lasting more than 72 hours. However, it's important to acknowledge that experiencing DOMS is normal as you advance on your fitness journey.

Cardio

Prior to engaging in regular pickleball play, it is essential to establish an adequate baseline level of cardiovascular fitness. The good news is, pickleball isn't all that strenuous on the cardiovascular system relative to other sports. For most active individuals, jumping straight in should not be a problem.

As mentioned with regards to pacing, even completely inactive people can gradually increase their cardio over time to moderate-intensity activity, such as pickleball, without any known risk of sudden cardiac events.[12] The cardiovascular demand of pickleball was established in a study by Smith et al. by having participants wear monitors to track cardiac response to pickleball play. The study determined pickleball to be "moderate intensity" based on established intensity guidelines.[13]

In the exercise science world, we use METs to compare the relative intensity of different activities. A MET, which stands for metabolic equivalent of task, is a measure of energy expended during physical activity compared to energy expended at rest. 1 MET is the amount of energy expended when sitting quietly. For instance, treadmill and regular walking at 3.0 miles per hour is a "moderate intensity" physical activity at 3.3 METs.

Moderate-intensity physical activity in metabolic terms has been classified as 3 to 6 METs. In the study conducted, it was found that playing doubles pickleball resulted in an absolute exercise intensity of 4.1 ± 1.0 METs.[13] The participants' heart rates increased to 40-60% of their heart rate reserve during the activity[13] For a list of activities with comparable METs to pickleball, see Table 6 below.

Table 6. Activities and Their MET Equivalents	
3 METs	Walking on a flat surface for one or two blocks
4 METs	Raking leaves, weeding or pushing a power mower, walking up two flights of stairs, doubles pickleball
5 METs	Walking four miles per hour, social dancing, washing a car
6 METs	Nine holes of golf carrying clubs, heavy carpentry or using a push mower

Adapted from Weinstein, 2018.[73]

Research is quite clear that for most individuals, the benefits of low-to-moderate intensity exercise substantially outweighs any risks; however, for a small segment (i.e., high risk) of the population, the risk of exercise-related events such as a heart attack or sudden death, is substantial when performing bouts of exercise their body is unaccustomed to, in particular vigorous intensity exercises. If you have a history of high-risk cardiac disease, participating in pickleball may pose excessive strain and could potentially jeopardize your safety. Most likely, anyone in this category would never dream of playing as they are far too ill and deconditioned to consider it.

If you are entirely deconditioned, jumping straight into full pickleball play for a few hours is not recommended. Begin by ramping up a walking program until you can walk for 30 minutes straight at a brisk pace. Once at this level, you should be able to make further progress in your cardiovascular fitness with regular pickleball playing, by gradually and progressively ramping up total play time.

Mobility

Mobility refers to the ability of our joints to move freely through their full, normal range of motion. It's an essential component of fitness that is often overlooked but it plays a crucial role in preventing injuries. Maintaining adequate mobility as we age helps prevent injuries by improving joint health and reducing the risk of muscle strains and sprains. When your joints are appropriately mobile, they are better able to absorb impact and distribute force, reducing the strain on adjacent joints as well as your muscles and tendons. This makes it less likely that you'll suffer an injury during physical activity.

Take for example the ankle joint—more specifically the talocrural joint of the ankle.

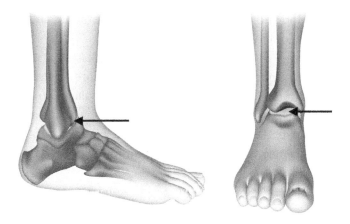

When the talocrural joint is stiff, say due to swelling after an ankle sprain or immobility after wearing a walking boot, our ability to dorsiflex the foot is reduced. Ankle dorsiflexion is the ability to flex your foot upward towards your shin. Limited ankle dorsiflexion causes compensations in the movement patterns of the foot, ankle, and knee and can lead to altered gait mechanics, overuse injuries, and pain in the lower leg particularly in activities such as squatting, lunging, and running. For example, if the ankle joint cannot move freely during a squat or a jump, the knee may compensate by moving inward, which can increase the risk of knee injuries.[74] Talocrural joint stiffness is a known risk factor for development of anterior knee pain, plantar fasciitis, Achilles tendinitis, and lateral ankle sprains.[75-77]

Pickleball is a sport that requires a certain level of joint mobility. When lacking it, our bodies will follow the path of least resistance and develop compensatory strategies. There are several key areas that should be addressed to keep you on the court for a lifetime of pain-free pickleball: ankle dorsiflexion, knee flexion and extension, hip and spine rotation, and global shoulder mobility.

Looking to improve your mobility? There are several exercises and techniques that can help. Foam rolling, stretching, and dynamic warm-up exercises are all great ways to improve joint mobility. Below is my personal list of the top 8 mobility drills to maintain and improve joint mobility necessary for pickleball.

Pickleball Mobility Exercises

1. Achilles stretch
2. Heel elevated deep squat
3. Foot elevated deep lunge
4. Discos
5. Shoulder circles
6. Sleeper stretch
7. Pec doorway stretch
8. World's greatest stretch

Achilles Stretch (Ankle Dorsiflexion)

This stretch is designed to help improve ankle dorsiflexion mobility as well as flexibility of our calf muscles (gastrocnemius and soleus).

1. Start by standing facing a wall with your hands placed on the wall at shoulder height.
2. Place one foot approximately 12 inches away from the wall and the other foot behind you.
3. Keeping your back leg straight and your heel on the ground, bend your front knee and lean forward towards the wall, allowing your knee to move towards the wall.
4. Continue to lean forward until you feel a stretch in your calf and ankle.
5. Hold the stretch for 20-30 seconds, then switch legs and repeat.
6. Aim to do this stretch daily, holding for longer periods of time as you progress.

Heel Elevated Deep Squat

The heel elevated squat is an exercise that can help improve knee and hip mobility and flexibility, as well as strengthen the lower body muscles.

1. Stand with your feet shoulder-width apart and place your heels on a small platform such as a weight plate, wooden dowel, or a stable block.
2. Position your toes straight forward, or pointed out to the side, whichever is more comfortable.
3. Place your arms out in front or hold a weight in front of your chest.
4. Slowly lower your body down towards the ground, bending at the knees and hips, taking your joints to the end of their comfortable range, not beyond it.
5. Aim to get your thighs parallel to the ground, or as low as you can go with minimal discomfort.
6. Push through your heels to stand back up to the starting position.
7. Aim to complete 10 repetitions.

Foot Elevated Deep Lunge

Commonly referred to as a deep split squat, this exercise targets the quads, hamstrings, and glutes, while also improving flexibility in the hips, knees, and ankles. Here's how to perform the deep lunge:

1. Start by standing with one foot forward on a step and the other foot back, in a split stance.
2. Lower your body down towards the ground by bending your front knee as much as possible with your front knee drifting over your toes and keeping your back knee straight.
3. Aim to get your back knee as close to the ground as possible while keeping the back knee straight.
4. As you lower your body, keep your torso upright.
5. Pause at the bottom of the movement and hold for a few seconds.
6. Push through your front foot to return to the starting position.
7. Aim to complete 5-10 repetitions on one side before switching to the other side.
8. If this is painful, or too challenging, elevate the front foot higher. If it is too easy, reduce the height of the front foot or perform on the floor.

Disco

The Disco is a mobility exercise designed to improve rotation through your spine and hips, which is tricky to maintain as we age and necessary for pickleball.

1. Stand upright with both feet pointing straight ahead.
2. Begin reaching to the right with your left hand, keeping the toes of your right foot pointing straight ahead, allowing your left foot to pivot to the right.
3. Reach as far as you can to the right, rotating through your trunk and right hip as far as you can. Reach directly across, rather than behind you.
4. Repeat the movement ten times, then switch sides and perform the movement by reaching to the left using your right arm.

* Variation—reaching across and up, or across and down can be helpful to work out any specific areas of tightness.

Standard Disco   Diagonal Variation

Shoulder Circles

Full shoulder circles can help improve shoulder mobility and flexibility, making it easier to hit overhead balls, or shots that are just out of reach.

1. Start by standing with your feet shoulder-width apart and your arms hanging down by your sides.
2. Slowly raise one arm forward and up towards the ceiling, keeping your thumb pointed up.
3. Once the arm is overhead, rotate your trunk towards that arm and begin lowering your arm back down to the waist, still with your thumb facing up. This movement is similar to doing the backstroke when you're swimming.
4. To perform a forward shoulder circle, simply begin with trunk rotation toward the moving arm, lead with your thumb facing upward and once overhead lower the arm back down towards the waist.
5. Aim to complete 10-20 circles with each arm in each direction.

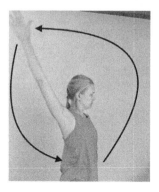

Sleeper Stretch

The sleeper stretch is a popular exercise that can help improve shoulder mobility and flexibility. Do not force the stretch or take the stretch beyond a stretching discomfort into pain. Once stretching is completed, there should be no lingering soreness. The sleeper stretch is a useful mobility exercise if you experience tightness or limited range of motion in your shoulder.

1. Lie on your side directly on your shoulder.
2. Bend your elbow to 90 degrees and rest it on the ground in front of your body.
3. Use your other hand to gently push your wrist towards the ground, until you feel a stretch in your shoulder.
4. Hold the stretch for 15-30 seconds.
5. Release the stretch and repeat on the other side.
6. Aim to perform 2-3 sets of 15-30 second holds on each side.

Doorway Stretch

This is an excellent stretch that incorporates both pec flexibility and thoracic extension. It is a useful mobility exercise for those who experience tightness or limited range of motion in their chest or upper back, such as those who spend a lot of time sitting or hunched over a computer. Here's how to perform the doorway stretch:

1. Stand in a doorway and place your forearms on the door frame at shoulder height, with your elbows bent at a 90-degree angle.
2. Take a small step forward with one foot, keeping your elbows and forearms in contact with the door frame.
3. Slowly lean forward, allowing your chest to move through the doorway while keeping your elbows and forearms in contact with the door frame.
4. Hold the stretch for 15-30 seconds, a stretch should be felt in your chest and upper back.
5. Return to the starting position and repeat on the other side.
6. Aim to perform 2-3 sets of 20-30 second holds on each side.

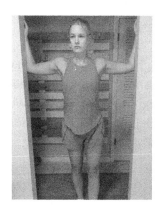

If the doorway stretch is too challenging or painful for you, try these modifications:

1. Adjust the height of your arms: If the stretch is too difficult with your arms at shoulder height, try raising or lowering your arms to find a more comfortable position.
2. Use a narrower doorway: If the doorway is too wide, it may be difficult to keep your elbows and forearms in contact with the door frame. Try using a narrower doorway or placing your hands on the walls in a corner instead.
3. Reduce the range of motion: If you can't lean forward very far without feeling discomfort, try reducing the range of motion by only leaning forward slightly or holding the stretch for a shorter period of time.

World's Greatest Stretch

The "World's Greatest" stretch is a dynamic mobility drill that targets the spine, hips, hamstrings, and shoulders. It can be incorporated into a warm-up routine before a workout or performed as a standalone exercise. Here's how to perform the "World's Greatest" stretch:

1. Start in a high plank position with your hands directly under your shoulders and your feet hip-width apart.
2. Step your right foot forward between your hands.
3. Keep your left hand on the ground and reach your right arm up towards the ceiling, rotating your torso to the right.

4. Hold the stretch for a few seconds, then bring your right hand back down to the ground.
5. Keep your right hand on the ground and reach your left arm up towards the ceiling, rotating your torso to the left.
6. Return to the high plank position and repeat on the other side, stepping your left foot forward between your hands.
7. Aim to perform 1-2 sets of 5-10 repetitions on each side.

Mobility is a critical part of fitness that plays a vital role in preventing injuries. By improving joint health and reducing the risk of muscle strains and sprains, mobility exercises can help you stay injury-free and achieve your fitness goals. As a pickleball athlete, make sure to prioritize mobility drills by adding them to your workout routine.

CHAPTER 5

POSTGAME RECOVERY

Cool down

Many opinions and debates exist in the exercise-science world regarding proper cool down and recovery after exercise. The physiological benefits of immediate postgame cool downs are grossly overexaggerated, particularly when conveyed by social media influencers looking to give you an additional video to like. Unfortunately, cooling down after exercise does not help to reduce muscle soreness, nor does it reduce the chance of injury.[78]

Cooldowns do, however, help you reduce your heart rate more slowly than just stopping abruptly and either sitting or lying down. Interestingly, heart problems tend to happen more frequently in the post-exercise recovery period than they do during play. So, if your heart rate is quite high after a tough game, you'll want to bring it back down by walking a few laps around the court.

The amount of time you spend cooling down is going to be different for everyone. It depends on how strenuous your matches were and how long it takes your body to get back to normal.

Recovery

Recovery after pickleball is important, particularly if you plan to play over consecutive days. The below tips for recovery will be helpful as you prepare for your next match:

- **Stretching/Mobility**. I recommend spending at least a few minutes at the conclusion of play to stretch any areas of tightness or going through mobility drills listed in Chapter 4 that pertain to any specific injuries you may be dealing with.
- **Refuel.** When we exercise or train, we are putting stress on our body. Our muscles, tendons, ligaments, and entire physiology are working hard for us, which is great, but this also means we need to ensure that we are recovering properly afterward. We spend energy when we exercise, so we want to get a jump-start on replenishing this soon after training.

  According to Jillian Tholen, a Registered Dietitian and Sports Nutritionist, our top priorities after completing a pickleball competition or practice should be focused on carbohydrate intake and ensuring proper hydration.[79] Research tells us that right after exercise, our muscles can use carbohydrates even more efficiently than usual, and these really help to start the recovery process for the whole body.

Opting for a small, high-carb snack within 30-45 minutes of concluding your game can have a significant impact. Examples of suitable food options include simple granola bars or fig bars, bananas, dry cereal, and pretzels. These choices can help replenish your energy levels effectively.

In terms of protein consumption, immediate intake after exercise is not necessarily crucial. However, it is important to ensure an adequate amount of protein in your next meal, preferably within two hours of completing your competition. Protein sources can vary from eggs, tofu, or cheese to meats like chicken or beef, and even options such as Greek yogurt or cottage cheese. The objective is to incorporate protein into your meals to provide your muscles with the necessary nutrients for recovery and repair purposes.

Finally, it's important to eat enough food when you are not playing or practicing. Fuel is important for helping with fitness, recovery, and overall health, so do your best to eat consistent meals and snacks during the day, and ensure you are eating when you are hungry. Getting enough calories is one of the most important considerations around sports nutrition.

- **Hydrate.** Most athletes finish exercise at a fluid deficit and will need to rehydrate to return to normal homeostasis. Effective rehydration requires the intake of a greater volume of fluid (125%–150%) than the final fluid deficit. ACSM recommends 1.25–1.5 L fluid for every 1 kg of body weight lost.[28]
- **Avoid Excessive Alcohol.** Excessive post-exercise alcohol consumption is discouraged as alcohol has diuretic effects and may impede rehydration

attempts. This may be a challenge for some with the rising popularity of pickleball bars and distilleries with attached pickleball courts. Be responsible and drink in moderation.

- **Relative Rest**. If your body is telling you that playing again later today, or even tomorrow is too soon, don't push your luck and jump back on the court too quickly. Take some time off and let your body recover. This does not mean you have to lie around on the couch and watch Netflix, but does mean that switching out pickleball for a long run or playing a different sport is likely not giving yourself time to recover. You may, however, continue with some easy exercise during a resting phase.

  It is particularly helpful to include light aerobic activity (cycling, swimming, walking) and strength training (machines or free weights) on days when you are not playing pickleball. Light aerobic activity can help with DOMS and joint soreness/stiffness, aiding in recovery and making you more prepared for your next pickleball games.

CHAPTER 6

INJURIES AND WHAT TO DO ABOUT THEM

Despite its relatively low impact and slower pace compared to other racket sports, injuries in pickleball are not entirely avoidable. By following the guidance in this book, taking action to start a strength training routine, and pacing yourself appropriately to allow for tissue adaptation, your risk for injury will be dramatically less.

If you or a partner do get injured while playing, following these general guidelines based on injury severity will be a great place to start.

Minor Injuries

Determining the severity of an injury can be challenging for someone who is not medically trained, but there are a few signs that would indicate a minor injury:

- **Pain:** Minor injuries typically result in mild to moderate pain that is manageable and doesn't significantly affect your daily activities. The pain is usually localized and doesn't radiate to other areas.
- **Swelling:** Minor injuries may cause minor swelling around the affected area. The swelling is usually limited and doesn't spread extensively.
- **Range of Motion:** You can typically move the injured body part with some discomfort but without significant restriction. There may be slight stiffness or reduced range of motion, but it is not severe.
- **Bruising:** Minor injuries might result in minor bruising, often in the form of small, localized bruises around the injury site. The bruising is usually not extensive nor widespread.

For minor injuries, the mnemonic to remember for the initial treatment is POLICE: Protect, Optimal Loading, Ice, Compression, and Elevation. The POLICE principle is a modern first aid method of treating musculoskeletal injuries. It promotes safe and effective loading in acute soft tissue injuries which is more effective than bedrest.

Protection of an injury such as a strain or sprain may be necessary in the acute phases due to the pain and/or risk of worsening the injury. Optimal loading refers to finding the ideal amount of stress to be applied to the injured area while it is healing. Optimal loading will stimulate the injured tissues to heal at a faster rate than complete immobilization.

In mild injuries, loading can usually be guided by one's pain experience and may need to be modified with the use of mobility aids such as crutches, braces, etc. in order to sufficiently unload and support the tissues in the early phases of recovery.

Here's an example: a patient of mine, Jen, sprained her ankle playing pickleball wearing old, loose tennis shoes. She had planted her foot funny, and her ankle rolled out to the side resulting in a low-grade ankle sprain with immediate pain, swelling, and mild bruising. In the clinic, Jen was having a very tough time walking on her injured ankle without a substantial limp. I was able to provide Jen with a set of crutches in order normalize her gait pattern, encourage mobility of the ankle joint, and allow the calf muscles to squeeze swelling/fluid out of the lower leg as she walked. Overprotecting the joint by locking the ankle in a boot/cast or advising her to avoid using the injured ankle would have hindered her recovery.

Icing may also be helpful in the early phase of an injury for pain control and swelling reduction. Compression via an ACE wrap, compression garment, etc. will also help mitigate swelling and improve stability of the involved joints. And finally, elevation is recommended to reduce swelling. To ensure the elevation is sufficient, make sure that the involved body part is elevated higher than your heart.

Moderate Injury

Moderate injuries as compared to mild ones, will often be characterized by more pronounced pain and more noticeable swelling or bruising. You will have less range of motion and more stiffness that may impede your ability to move the injured body part freely. Moderate injuries can significantly impact not just your ability to play pickleball, but also your capacity to carry out everyday tasks, with noticeable limitations.

If you experience a moderate injury on the court or are dealing with a non-improving sprain or strain, you should be formally assessed by an orthopedic professional. A physical therapist or an orthopedic or sports medicine physician is best suited to aid in diagnosing and managing your injury. Oftentimes lingering symptoms are not the result of a single problematic area, but may be due to movement compensations, overtraining, inadequate range of motion, poor strength, or any number of extraneous variables. A thorough examination by your healthcare provider will clarify the root cause of your problem and determine a treatment path towards recovery.

Severe Injury

Unfortunately, these injuries can and do occur, albeit on a less frequent basis. A severe injury will typically present with intense pain and may include deformity or visible damage such as in the case of joint dislocation or fracture. Inability to bear weight on the affected limb or presence of excessive swelling or bruising is also a sign of a more serious injury.

Management of severe injuries is outside the scope of this book. One should be aware of the closest Automated External Defibrillator (AED) in case of a cardiac event such as a heart attack and have access to a telephone to call 911 if symptoms indicate a significant or life-threatening problem.

CONCLUSION

Pickleball is an incredible sport and is taking the country by storm. Data suggest this is not a fad that will pass quickly, but rather an emerging sport that is here to stay. As with any sport, there is always a risk of injury. For nearly everyone, the numerous physical, mental, and social benefits of playing pickleball far outweigh any associated risks involved with the sport. The good news is that by following the injury prevention techniques provided in this book you can significantly reduce the likelihood of getting injured and ensure the long-term enjoyment of pickleball well into your later years.

Here is a recap of my top 10 strategies and recommendations to prevent injuries. Now it's time for you to put them into action.

1. Address physical impairments that have been nagging you for some time. This may simply mean targeting areas of weakness by beginning the strengthening exercises or improving a mobility deficit by adding the mobility drills listed in this book to your workout routine. For others it may mean you need to start with a formal check-up with your medical doctor or physical therapist.

2. Train for the sport. Injury prevention happens off the court. Tissue resilience is made in the weight room.

3. Warm-up before you play. Be the odd man out who actually warms up before playing. Doing 20 dinks from the kitchen will have no effect on injury prevention, but a warm-up that gets your heart rate up and gets blood pumping in your shoulders and legs has potential to pay dividends.

4. Use the proper gear. Consider investing in things like pickleball shoes, protective eyewear, and a good paddle.

5. Listen to your body. It is perfectly normal to feel like a million dollars one day, and then incredibly sluggish the next. Some days our body is ready for action, firing on all cylinders and can handle a shocking amount of physical stress. On these days, it is perfectly ok to play a few more games, drive and spike a bit harder than usual.

   An extensive number of secondary and tertiary factors can contribute to "bad days" in your training. Frequently, this can be from poor recovery after your last pickleball session. Consider how well you are taking care of your body. Key things to consider include sleep, stress (work, family, etc.), nutrition and hydration status, and tissue overload from other activities, such as helping a friend move the day before. Refer to Chapter 1 for more details on this.

6. Know your limits for that given day. When playing in warmer weather, higher humidity, or full sun, your limits need to adjust. Is this the 4th day in a row you're playing for two hours? You may need more rest between games or a day off for full recovery.

7. Play smarter not harder—pay attention to your body position and footwork.

8. Improve your game. The better pickleball player you are, the less diving, sprinting after the ball, running backwards, etc. you will have to do. You will be better able to predict where the ball is going and move ahead of time. Practice, practice, practice and your reaction times will speed up, making you less vulnerable to taking risky, reachy shots.

9. Pace yourself. I know you love the game. We all do, but seriously look back and estimate the percent increase in volume you are making as you begin to play more. You may need to gradually ramp up instead of doubling or tripling the amount of time on the court each week. This is where I see overuse injuries happen the most.

10. Play more consistently. Sporadic or inconsistent pickleball is a common reason someone might find themselves dealing with pain or injury. Every time you play, new stress will be placed upon your weight bearing joints (ankles, knees, hips, lower back) as well as your shoulder joints and all the muscles that support these areas.

With inconsistent play, particularly when the infrequent bouts are intense or long in duration, you are essentially starting over again on building up your tissue capacity, which can increase your risk for pain or injury. It's better to develop a reasonably consistent play strategy. If you aren't playing consistently, physiological adaptations to the sport will not occur (joint impact tolerance, strength improvements, balance and coordination, etc.)

A simple recommendation is to start playing more. Begin with two non-consecutive days/week, then build to three days/week, then four or more if you have the time.

Thank you for embarking on this journey with me and investing your time in reading my book, "Pain-Free Pickleball." It has been an honor to share my knowledge and insights with you, and I sincerely hope that you have found valuable information within its pages.

Your commitment to learning and your dedication to staying injury-free in the game of pickleball are commendable. By taking the initiative to empower yourself with the tools and knowledge provided in this comprehensive guide, you have demonstrated your passion for the sport and your desire to thrive on the court.

To unlock exclusive bonus content, access additional resources, and stay updated with the latest tips and strategies for injury prevention and optimal performance in pickleball, visit my website at www.pain-freepickleball.com. Discover in-depth guides, video tutorials, and join a vibrant community of pickleball enthusiasts dedicated to staying injury-free and thriving on the court.

I am grateful for the opportunity to make a positive impact on the pickleball community through this book. It is my utmost goal to see players of all ages and skill levels flourish and enjoy the game they love without the burden of injuries. Your engagement and commitment to implementing the practices and strategies outlined in this book will contribute to a stronger, healthier pickleball community overall.

Remember, your journey toward injury prevention and optimal performance doesn't end here. Stay curious, keep seeking knowledge, and continue implementing the principles shared in this book. Together, we can create a culture of thriving and longevity in pickleball.

Once again, thank you for joining me on this quest for pain-free pickleball. Your dedication and passion inspire me, and I wish you many joyful and fulfilling moments on the court. Keep playing, keep growing, and may your pickleball journey be filled with excitement, camaraderie, and countless victories.

With heartfelt gratitude,
Dr. Trent Stensrud, DPT, OCS, FAAOMPT

6-WEEK CHALLENGE!

Now, it's time to put all the knowledge you've gained into action. Preparation off the court is an essential part of preventing injuries on the court, so I invite you to take on this 6-week pickleball exercise challenge. The challenge is designed to gradually increase your fitness level and help you set up a consistent workout routine. Remember to consult with a healthcare professional before starting any new exercise program.

Week 1: Establishing the Foundation

Goal: Build a solid foundation and set up a workout routine.

1. Pickleball: Start the 10-minute warm up before play listed in Chapter 2. Purchase some good court shoes if you have not yet done so.
2. Strength Training: Complete two non-consecutive days of weight training using the Day 1 and Day 2 exercises listed in Chapter 4. Aim for a single set of 8-12 reps for each exercise at a 4-5/10 RPE level.
3. Mobility: Spend at least 10 minutes stretching and improving your flexibility after each workout.

Week 2: Building Strength

Goal: Improve muscular strength and endurance.

1. Pickleball: Continue with the dynamic warm-up and add in practicing pickleball shots before play.
2. Strength Training: Add an additional set for each exercise. Continue with Day 1 and Day 2 lifting schedules for a total of two days/week, begin to increase the weight or difficulty of exercises to moderate or 5-6/10 RPE.
3. Mobility: Spend at least 10 minutes stretching and improving your mobility after each workout using exercises provided in Chapter 4.

Week 3: Enhancing Endurance

Goal: Boost muscle endurance and continue building strength.

1. Pickleball: Continue with the dynamic warm up and practicing pickleball shots before play.
2. Strength Training: Increase the number of sets to three for each exercise and focus on increasing the weight or difficulty. The goal is 5-6/10 RPE.
3. Mobility: Spend at least 10 minutes stretching and improving your mobility after each workout using exercises provided in Chapter 4. Devote more time to any problem areas that arise during play.

Week 4: Progressive Overload

Goal: Increase the intensity of your strength training sessions.

1. Pickleball: Continue with the dynamic warm up and practicing pickleball shots before play.
2. Progressive Overload: Increase the weight or resistance used for each exercise by approximately 5-10%. You should be reaching a 7/10 RPE level after each set. Continue with three sets for each exercise.
3. Mobility: Spend at least 10 minutes stretching and improving your mobility after each workout using exercises provided in Chapter 4. Devote more time to any problem areas that arise during play.

Week 5: Intensifying the Effort

Goal: Increase the intensity and variety of your workouts.

1. Pickleball: Continue with the dynamic warm up and practicing pickleball shots before play.
2. Strength Training: Add in a third day of resistance training into your routine using the Day 3 template listed in Chapter 4. Increase the weight or difficulty as needed to keep a 7/10 RPE level after each set.
3. Mobility: Spend at least 10 minutes stretching and improving your mobility after each workout using exercises provided in Chapter 4. Devote more time to any problem areas that arise during play.

Week 6: Sustaining the Lifestyle

Goal: Maintain your progress and establish a lifelong commitment to fitness.

1. Pickleball: Continue with the dynamic warm up and practicing pickleball shots before play. Maintain your current play schedule without a long hiatus between games.
2. Strength Training: Continue with the three-day lifting program. Focus on refining your technique and aim for progressive overload by gradually increasing the weight or difficulty when able.
3. Mobility: Continue to spend time daily to maintain mobility improvements gained over these past 6 weeks. Continue to work on improving mobility impairments that arise going forward.

Remember, this 6-week challenge is just the beginning of your pickleball fitness and injury prevention journey. As you progress, continue challenging yourself, setting new goals, and exploring different exercises and techniques to further enhance your strength and overall fitness. Stay consistent, listen to your body, and enjoy the process of becoming a more resilient human!

URGENT PLEA!

Thank You for Reading My Book!

I'd really appreciate your feedback and
I'd love to hear what you have to say.

I need your input to make the next version of
this book and my future books even better.

Please take two minutes now to leave a helpful review on
Amazon letting me know what you thought of the book:
Pain-freepickleball.com/review

Thanks so much!
—Trent

SOURCES

1. *Pickleball history: Pickleball origin.* USA Pickleball. (2023, April 10). https://usapickleball.org/what-is-pickleball/history-of-the-game/

2. Sports & Fitness Industry Association's (SFIA). 2019 Pickleball Participant Report, from the 2019 Physical Activity Council Sports, Fitness, and Recreational Activity Study. Silver Spring: Tennis Industry Association; 2019.

3. Goldon, Jessica. "Pickleball Popularity Exploded Last Year With More Than 36.5 Million Playing the Sport". CNBC, 5 Jan 2023. https://www.cnbc.com/2023/01/05/pickleball-popularity-explodes-with-more-than-36-million-playing.html

4. Callahan, John, and Charlie Cai. *Pickleball: Tips, Strategies, Lessons, & Myths from a Certified Pickleball Professional & U. S. Open Gold Medal Winner.* Callahan Pickleball Academy, 2020.

5. Weiss, H., Dougherty, J., & DiMaggio, C. (2021). Non-fatal senior pickleball and tennis-related injuries treated in United States emergency departments, 2010–2019. *Injury epidemiology*, 8(1), 1-15.

6. Forrester M. B. (2020). Pickleball-Related Injuries Treated in Emergency Departments. *The Journal of emergency medicine*, 58(2), 275–279. https://doi.org/10.1016/j.jemermed.2019.09.016

7. Maffulli N, Sharma P, Luscombe KL. Achilles tendinopathy: aetiology and management. J R Soc Med. 2004;97(10):472-476. doi:10.1258/jrsm.97.10.472

8. Kannus P, Józsa L. Histopathological changes preceding spontaneous rupture of a tendon. A controlled study of 891 patients. J Bone Joint Surg Am. 1991;73(10):1507-1525. doi:10.2106/00004623-199173100-00006

[9] Cook JL, Purdam CR. Is tendon pathology a continuum? A pathology model to explain the clinical presentation of load-induced tendinopathy. Br J Sports Med. 2009;43(6):409-416. doi:10.1136/bjsm.2008.051193

[10] Khan KM, Cook JL, Kannus P, Maffulli N, Bonar SF. Time to abandon the "tendinitis" myth. BMJ. 2002;324(7338):626-627. doi:10.1136/bmj.324.7338.626

[11] Ritchel, M. (2022, Aug 22) Pickleball, Sport of the Future Injury? New York Times. https://www.nytimes.com/2022/08/20/health/pickleball-sports-injury.html

[12] Piercy, K. L., Troiano, R. P., Ballard, R. M., Carlson, S. A., Fulton, J. E., Galuska, D. A., ... & Olson, R. D. (2018). The physical activity guidelines for Americans. *Jama, 320*(19), 2020-2028.

[13] Smith, L. E., Buchanan, C. A., & Dalleck, L. C. (2018). The acute and chronic physiological responses to pickleball in middle-aged and older adults. *International Journal of Research in Exercise Physiology, 13*(2), 21-32.

[14] Blackwell, D. L., & Clarke, T. C. (2018). State variation in meeting the 2008 federal guidelines for both aerobic and muscle-strengthening activities through leisure-time physical activity among adults aged 18-64: United States, 2010-2015. *National health statistics reports,* (112), 1-22.

[15] World Health Organization. (2017). *Depression and other common mental disorders: global health estimates* (No. WHO/MSD/MER/2017.2). World Health Organization.

[16] Goodwin, R. D., Dierker, L. C., Wu, M., Galea, S., Hoven, C. W., & Weinberger, A. H. (2022). Trends in U.S. Depression Prevalence From 2015 to 2020: The Widening Treatment Gap. *American journal of preventive medicine, 63*(5), 726–733. https://doi.org/10.1016/j.amepre.2022.05.014

[17] Heo, J., Ryu, J., Yang, H., Kim, A. C. H., & Rhee, Y. (2018). Importance of playing pickleball for older adults' subjective well-being: A serious leisure perspective. The Journal of Positive Psychology, 13(1), 67-77.

[18] Heo, J., Ryu, J., Yang, H., & Kim, K. M. (2018). Serious leisure and depression in older adults: A study of pickleball players. *Leisure Studies, 37*(5), 561-573.

[19] Buzzelli, A. A., & Draper, J. A. (2019). Examining the motivation and perceived benefits of pickleball participation

in older adults. Journal of Aging and Physical Activity, 28(2), 180-186.

20 Perissinotto, C., Holt-Lunstad, J., Periyakoil, V. S., & Covinsky, K. (2019). A practical approach to assessing and mitigating loneliness and isolation in older adults. Journal of the American Geriatrics Society, 67(4), 657–662. https://doi.org/10.1111/jgs.15746

21 National Academies of Sciences, Engineering, and Medicine. (2020). Social isolation and loneliness in older adults: Opportunities for the health care system. Washington, DC: The National Academies Press. https://doi.org/10.17226/25663

22 Holt-Lunstad, J., Smith, T. B., & Layton, J. B. (2010). Social relationships and mortality risk: A meta-analytic review. PLoS Medicine, 7(7), e1000316. https://doi.org/10.1371/journal.pmed.1000316

23 Holt-Lunstad, J., Smith, T. B., Baker, M., Harris, T., & Stephenson, D. (2015). Loneliness and social isolation as risk factors for mortality: A meta-analytic review. Perspectives on Psychological Science, 10(2), 227–237. https://doi.org/10.1177/1745691614568352

24 Liechty, T., Genoe, M.R., & Marston, H.R. (2017). Physically active leisure and the transition to retirement: The value of context. Annals of Leisure Research, 20(1), 23–38. doi:10.1080/11745398.2016.

25 Ryu, J., Yang, H., Kim, A. C. H., Kim, K. M., & Heo, J. (2018). Understanding pickleball as a new leisure pursuit among older adults. Educational Gerontology, 44(2-3), 128-138.

26 Casper, J. M., & Jeon, J. H. (2018). Psychological connection to pickleball: Assessing motives and participation in older adults. Journal of aging and physical activity, 27(1), 28-33.

27 Cerezuela JL, Lirola MJ, Cangas AJ. Pickleball and mental health in adults: A systematic review. Front Psychol. 2023 Feb 21;14:1137047. doi: 10.3389/fpsyg.2023.1137047. PMID: 36895753; PMCID: PMC9988900

28 Thomas, D. T., Erdman, K. A., & Burke, L. M. (2016). Position of the Academy of Nutrition and Dietetics, Dietitians of Canada, and the American College of Sports Medicine: nutrition and athletic performance. Journal of the Academy of Nutrition and Dietetics, 116(3), 501-528.

[29] Vitale, K., & Liu, S. (2020). Pickleball: review and clinical recommendations for this fast-growing sport. *Current sports medicine reports, 19*(10), 406-413.

[30] Bouché, R. T. (2017). Court Shoes and Orthoses for Racquet Sports: Tennis, Pickleball, Badminton, Squash, Racquetball, and American Handball. Athletic Footwear and Orthoses in Sports Medicine, 315-328.

[31] Martin, R. L., Davenport, T. E., Fraser, J. J., Sawdon-Bea, J., Carcia, C. R., Carroll, L. A., ... & Carreira, D. (2021). Ankle stability and movement coordination impairments: Lateral ankle ligament sprains revision 2021: Clinical practice guidelines linked to the international classification of functioning, disability and health from the Academy of Orthopaedic Physical Therapy of the American Physical Therapy Association. *Journal of Orthopaedic & Sports Physical Therapy, 51*(4), CPG1-CPG80.

[32] Lucado, A. M., Day, J. M., Vincent, J. I., MacDermid, J. C., Fedorczyk, J., Grewal, R., ... & Beattie, P. F. (2022). Lateral Elbow Pain and Muscle Function Impairments: Clinical Practice Guidelines Linked to the International Classification of Functioning, Disability and Health from the Academy of Hand and Upper Extremity Physical Therapy and the Academy of Orthopaedic Physical Therapy of the American Physical Therapy Association. *Journal of Orthopaedic & Sports Physical Therapy, 52*(12), CPG1-CPG111.

[33] Ramsey, D. K., & Russell, M. E. (2009). Unloader braces for medial compartment knee osteoarthritis: implications on mediating progression. Sports Health, 1(5), 416-426.

[34] Gohal, C., Shanmugaraj, A., Tate, P., Horner, N. S., Bedi, A., Adili, A., & Khan, M. (2018). Effectiveness of valgus offloading knee braces in the treatment of medial compartment knee osteoarthritis: a systematic review. Sports health, 10(6), 500-514.

[35] Elliot, M. (2023, Jan 17). Personal communication [Personal interview].

[36] Atkinson, C. F., Patron, M. E., & Joondeph, B. C. (2020). Retinal tears due to pickleball injury. Retinal Cases & Brief Reports, 16(3), 312-313.

[37] Gauer, R. L., & Meyers, B. K. (2019). Heat-related illnesses. American family physician, 99(8), 482-489.

38 Barrow, M. W., & Clark, K. A. (1998). Heat-related illnesses. *American family physician*, *58*(3), 749–759.
39 Bricknell, M. C. M. (1995). Heat illness-a review of military experience (Part 1). JOURNAL-ROYAL ARMY MEDICAL CORPS, 141, 157-157.
40 Casa, D. J., DeMartini, J. K., Bergeron, M. F., Csillan, D., Eichner, E. R., Lopez, R. M., ... & Yeargin, S. W. (2015). National Athletic Trainers' Association position statement: exertional heat illnesses. *Journal of athletic training*, *50*(9), 986-1000.
41 ACS. Skin cancer, American Cancer Society, 2005. www. cancer.org.
42 Tempelhof, S., Rupp, S., & Seil, R. (1999). Age-related prevalence of rotator cuff tears in asymptomatic shoulders. *Journal of shoulder and elbow surgery*, *8*(4), 296-299.
43 Brinjikji, W., Luetmer, P. H., Comstock, B., Bresnahan, B. W., Chen, L. E., Deyo, R. A., ... & Jarvik, J. G. (2015). Systematic literature review of imaging features of spinal degeneration in asymptomatic populations. *American journal of neuroradiology*, *36*(4), 811-816.
44 Fisher JP, Hassan DT, O'Connor N. Minerva. BMJ 1995;310:70.
45 Mueller, M. J., & Maluf, K. S. (2002). Tissue adaptation to physical stress: a proposed "Physical Stress Theory" to guide physical therapist practice, education, and research. *Physical therapy*, *82*(4), 383-403.
46 Sallis, R. E. (2009). Exercise is medicine and physicians need to prescribe it! British journal of sports medicine, 43(1), 3-4.
47 Berryman, J. W. (2010). Exercise is medicine: a historical perspective. Current sports medicine reports, 9(4), 195-201.
48 Lally F, Crome P. Understanding frailty. Postgrad Med J 83: 16–20, 2007
49 Kryger, A. I., & Andersen, J. L. (2007). Resistance training in the oldest old: consequences for muscle strength, fiber types, fiber size, and MHC isoforms. *Scandinavian journal of medicine & science in sports*, *17*(4), 422-430
50 Fiatarone, M. A., Marks, E. C., Ryan, N. D., Meredith, C. N., Lipsitz, L. A., & Evans, W. J. (1990). High-intensity strength training in nonagenarians: effects on skeletal muscle. *Jama*, *263*(22), 3029-3034.

51 Peterson, M. D., Sen, A., & Gordon, P. M. (2011). Influence of resistance exercise on lean body mass in aging adults: a meta-analysis. *Medicine and science in sports and exercise*, *43*(2), 249.

52 Fiatarone, Maria A., Evelyn F. O'Neill, Nancy Doyle Ryan, Karen M. Clements, Guido R. Solares, Miriam E. Nelson, Susan B. Roberts, Joseph J. Kehayias, Lewis A. Lipsitz, and William J. Evans. "Exercise training and nutritional supplementation for physical frailty in very elderly people." *New England Journal of Medicine* 330, no. 25 (1994): 1769-1775.

53 Binder, E. F., Birge, S. J., Spina, R., Ehsani, A. A., Brown, M., Sinacore, D. R., & Kohrt, W. M. (1999). Peak aerobic power is an important component of physical performance in older women. *Journals of Gerontology Series A: Biomedical Sciences and Medical Sciences*, *54*(7), M353-M356.

54 Hakkinen, K., Kraemer, W. J., Pakarinen, A., Tripleltt-Mcbride, T., McBride, J. M., Häkkinen, A., ... & Newton, R. U. (2002). Effects of heavy resistance/power training on maximal strength, muscle morphology, and hormonal response patterns in 60-75-year-old men and women. *Canadian Journal of Applied Physiology*, *27*(3), 213-231.

55 Gonzalez, A. M., Mangine, G. T., Fragala, M. S., Stout, J. R., Beyer, K. S., Bohner, J. D., ... & Hoffman, J. R. (2014). Resistance training improves single leg stance performance in older adults. *Aging clinical and experimental research*, *26*, 89-92

56 Goodpaster, B. H., Chomentowski, P., Ward, B. K., Rossi, A., Glynn, N. W., Delmonico, M. J., ... & Newman, A. B. (2008). Effects of physical activity on strength and skeletal muscle fat infiltration in older adults: a randomized controlled trial. *Journal of applied physiology*, *105*(5), 1498-1503.

57 Evans, W. J. (2002). Effects of exercise on senescent muscle. *Clinical Orthopaedics and Related Research (1976-2007)*, *403*, S211-S220.

58 Dalsky, G. P., Stocke, K. S., Ehsani, A. A., SLATOPOLSKY, E., LEE, W. C., & BIRGE Jr, S. J. (1988). Weight-bearing exercise training and lumbar bone mineral content in postmenopausal women. *Annals of internal medicine*, *108*(6), 824-828.

[59] Marques, E. A., Mota, J., & Carvalho, J. (2012). Exercise effects on bone mineral density in older adults: a meta-analysis of randomized controlled trials. *Age, 34,* 1493-1515.

[60] Davidson, L. E., Hudson, R., Kilpatrick, K., Kuk, J. L., McMillan, K., Janiszewski, P. M., Lee, S., Lam, M., & Ross, R. (2009). Effects of exercise modality on insulin resistance and functional limitation in older adults: a randomized controlled trial. *Archives of internal medicine, 169*(2), 122–131. https://doi.org/10.1001/archinternmed.2008.558

[61] Hoffmann, T. C., Maher, C. G., Briffa, T., Sherrington, C., Bennell, K., Alison, J., ... & Glasziou, P. P. (2016). Prescribing exercise interventions for patients with chronic conditions. *Cmaj, 188*(7), 510-518.

[62] de Vreede, P. L., van Meeteren, N. L., Samson, M. M., Wittink, H. M., Duursma, S. A., & Verhaar, H. J. (2006). The effect of functional tasks exercise and resistance exercise on health-related quality of life and physical activity: A randomized controlled trial. *Gerontology, 53*(1), 12-20

[63] Cassilhas, R. C., Antunes, H. K. M., Tufik, S., & De Mello, M. T. (2010). Mood, anxiety, and serum IGF-1 in elderly men given 24 weeks of high resistance exercise. *Perceptual and Motor skills, 110*(1), 265-276.

[64] Chen, K. M., Kuo, C. C., Chang, Y. H., Huang, H. T., & Cheng, Y. Y. (2017). Resistance band exercises reduce depression and behavioral problems of wheelchair-bound older adults with dementia: a cluster-randomized controlled trial. *Journal of the American Geriatrics Society, 65*(2), 356-363.

[65] Zanuso, S., Sieverdes, J. C., Smith, N., Carraro, A., & Bergamin, M. (2012). The effect of a strength training program on affect, mood, anxiety, and strength performance in older individuals. *International Journal of Sport Psychology, 43*(1), 53.

[66] Spirduso, W. W., & Cronin, D. L. (2001). Exercise dose–response effects on quality of life and independent living in older adults. *Medicine & science in sports & exercise.*

[67] Silva, R. B., Eslick, G. D., & Duque, G. (2013). Exercise for falls and fracture prevention in long term care facilities: a systematic review and meta-analysis. *Journal of the American Medical Directors Association, 14*(9), 685-689.

[68] Shah, K., Armamento-Villareal, R., Parimi, N., Chode, S., Sinacore, D. R., Hilton, T. N., ... & Villareal, D. T. (2011).

Exercise training in obese older adults prevents increase in bone turnover and attenuates decrease in hip bone mineral density induced by weight loss despite decline in bone-active hormones. *Journal of Bone and Mineral Research, 26*(12), 2851-2859.

[69] Nelson ME, Fiatarone MA, Morganti CM, et al. Effects of high-intensity strength training on multiple risk factors for osteoporotic fractures. A randomized controlled trial. JAMA 272: 1909–1914, 1994

[70] Bweir, S., Al-Jarrah, M., Almalty, A. M., Maayah, M., Smirnova, I. V., Novikova, L., & Stehno-Bittel, L. (2009). Resistance exercise training lowers HbA1c more than aerobic training in adults with type 2 diabetes. *Diabetology & metabolic syndrome, 1,* 1-7.

[71] Zourdos, M. C., Klemp, A., Dolan, C., Quiles, J. M., Schau, K. A., Jo, E., ... & Blanco, R. (2016). Novel resistance training–specific rating of perceived exertion scale measuring repetitions in reserve. The Journal of Strength & Conditioning Research, 30(1), 267-275.

[72] Haff, G. G., & Triplett, N. T. (Eds.). (2015). *Essentials of strength training and conditioning 4th edition.* Human kinetics.

[73] Weinstein, A. S., Sigurdsson, M. I., & Bader, A. M. (2018). Comparison of preoperative assessment of patient's metabolic equivalents (mets) estimated from history versus measured by exercise cardiac stress testing. Anesthesiology Research and Practice, 2018.

[74] Willy, R. W., Hoglund, L. T., Barton, C. J., Bolgla, L. A., Scalzitti, D. A., Logerstedt, D. S., ... & Torburn, L. (2019). Patellofemoral pain: clinical practice guidelines linked to the international classification of functioning, disability and health from the academy of orthopaedic physical therapy of the American physical therapy association. *Journal of Orthopaedic & Sports Physical Therapy, 49*(9), CPG1-CPG95.

[75] Martin, R. L., Chimenti, R., Cuddeford, T., Houck, J., Matheson, J. W., McDonough, C. M., ... & Carcia, C. R. (2018). Achilles pain, stiffness, and muscle power deficits: midportion Achilles tendinopathy revision 2018: clinical practice guidelines linked to the International Classification of Functioning, Disability and Health From the Orthopaedic Section of the American

Physical Therapy Association. Journal of Orthopaedic & Sports Physical Therapy, 48(5), A1-A38.

[76] Martin, R. L., Davenport, T. E., Reischl, S. F., McPoil, T. G., Matheson, J. W., Wukich, D. K., ... & Godges, J. J. (2014). Heel pain—plantar fasciitis: revision 2014. Journal of Orthopaedic & Sports Physical Therapy, 44(11), A1-A33.

[77] Martin, R. L., Davenport, T. E., Paulseth, S., Wukich, D. K., Godges, J. J., Altman, R. D., ... & Zachazewski, J. (2013). Ankle stability and movement coordination impairments: ankle ligament sprains: clinical practice guidelines linked to the international classification of functioning, disability and health from the orthopaedic section of the American Physical Therapy Association. Journal of Orthopaedic & Sports Physical Therapy, 43(9), A1-A40.

[78] Law, R. Y., & Herbert, R. D. (2007). Warm-up reduces delayed-onset muscle soreness, but cool-down does not: a randomised controlled trial. Australian Journal of Physiotherapy, 53(2), 91-95.

[79] Tholen, J. (2023, May 10). Personal communication [Personal interview].

[80] Wroblewski, A. P., Amati, F., Smiley, M. A., Goodpaster, B., & Wright, V. (2011). Chronic exercise preserves lean muscle mass in masters athletes. The Physician and sportsmedicine, 39(3), 172–178.

GLOSSARY OF TERMS

1. Baseline: The boundary line at the back of the court, which marks the farthest point from the net.
2. Capacity: The ability of a tissue or structure within the body to withstand or tolerate external forces or loads without sustaining damage or injury. It represents the maximum level of stress or load that a tissue can endure before it reaches its breaking point.
3. Closed Face: A paddle position referring to the orientation of the paddle. The face is angled slightly downward, creating a closed angle between the face of the paddle and the ground.
4. Dink: A soft shot that is hit just over the net, often used in the kitchen or non-volley zone.
5. Delayed Onset Muscle Soreness (DOMS): A type of muscular pain that occurs 24-72 hours after engaging in physical activity.
6. Drive: A shot where a player hits the ball with a relatively flat trajectory and moderate power, aimed at driving the ball past the opponent or deep into their court.
7. Flat Face: A paddle position referring to the orientation of the paddle face where it is parallel to the ground, with no significant upward or downward tilt.

This position is used when players want to hit the ball with a more neutral trajectory, without adding much topspin or slice.

8. Ground Stroke: A shot where a player hits the ball after it has bounced on the ground, typically from a baseline or mid-court position, aiming to keep the ball in play and direct it towards the opponent's side of the court.

9. Kitchen: The non-volley zone found on both sides of the net. Players must not volley the ball while standing inside this area.

10. Load: The amount of force or stress applied to a particular tissue or structure within the body. It is the external force acting upon the tissue, which can lead to injury or damage if it exceeds the tissue's capacity to withstand that force.

11. Lob: A high, arcing shot that travels deep into the opponent's court, typically used to reset the point or create distance.

12. Metabolic equivalent of task (MET): A measure of energy expended during physical activity compared to energy expended at rest.

13. Mobility: The ability of an individual to move or perform physical activities with ease and without restrictions or limitations. It encompasses various aspects such as flexibility, range of motion, joint function, and muscular strength needed for functional movement.

14. Non-Volley Zone: The area on each side of the net that extends seven feet back from the net. Volleying is not allowed while standing inside this zone. Also known as the "kitchen."

15. Open Face: A paddle position referring to the orientation of the paddle face where the face is angled

slightly upward, creating an open angle between the face of the paddle and the ground.

16. Osteoarthritis: A degenerative joint disease characterized by the gradual breakdown of the protective cartilage that cushions the ends of bones within a joint.

17. Overhead Smash: A forceful shot where a player strikes the ball with a downward motion from an elevated position above the head.

18. Poach: When a player intercepts the ball hit to their partner's side of the court.

19. Progressive Overload: Principle in strength training and conditioning that involves gradually increasing the exercise intensity, duration, or volume to continually challenge the body and stimulate fitness improvements.

20. Rally: The exchange of shots between opposing players or teams.

21. Rating of Perceived Exertion (RPE): A measure of the overall difficulty of the exercise on a scale from 0 to 10 based on self-perception, with zero being the amount of physical challenge at rest and 10 being the most challenging exercise possible.

22. Repetitions in Reserve (RIR): A measure of how many reps an individual feels they could have performed before reaching muscle failure at the conclusion of a set.

23. Resistance Training: A form of exercise that involves using external resistance, such as weights, resistance bands, or bodyweight, to build strength, increase muscle mass, and improve overall physical fitness. Also known as strength training or weight training.

24. Sarcopenia: The decline of skeletal muscle tissue as we age leading to a decrease in tissue resilience and a vulnerability to injury

25. Tennis Elbow: Also known as lateral epicondylitis, a condition characterized by pain and inflammation of the wrist extensor tendons on the outer part of the elbow, typically caused by repetitive arm and wrist movements.

26. Third Shot Drop: A shot hit softly and with precision into the opponent's non-volley zone after the return of serve, as the third shot of the rally.

27. Tissue Adaptation: The physiological changes and remodeling that occur within a tissue in response to specific demands or stimuli placed upon it.

28. Transition Zone: The area on the court found between the non-volley zone (kitchen) and the baseline. It is sometimes called the mid-court or no-man's land.

29. Volley: Hitting the ball in the air before it bounces on the ground.

AUTHOR BIO

Dr. Trent Stensrud, DPT, OCS, FAAOMPT is a renowned physical therapist and a clinical expert in sports injury prevention and rehabilitation. Dr. Stensrud holds a Doctorate in Physical Therapy and is a board-certified specialist in orthopedics. As a Fellow of the American Academy of Orthopedic Manual Physical Therapists, he is highly regarded for his clinical achievements.

Recognizing the unique demands and potential risks associated with pickleball, Dr. Stensrud became determined to provide players with the knowledge and tools they need to prevent injuries and enjoy the game to the fullest. His extensive research and hands-on experience in treating pickleball-related injuries have made him an authority on the subject.

Working with athletes of all levels, Dr. Stensrud's contemporary approach combines evidence-based practices with personalized guidance. By combining his expertise in biomechanics, pain neuroscience, strength and conditioning, injury prevention, and rehabilitation, he has helped countless individuals recover from pickleball injuries.

"Pain-Free Pickleball" represents Dr. Stensrud's commitment to empowering pickleball players with the knowledge and tools they need to stay injury-free. By sharing his expertise and insights in this comprehensive guide, he aims to make a positive impact on the pickleball community and help players of all ages and skill levels thrive in the game they love.

Outside of his work, Dr. Stensrud enjoys playing pickleball and resides in Minneapolis, MN with his wife and three children. He continues to advocate for aging well with pickleball.

Made in the USA
Las Vegas, NV
13 December 2024